Soft Words and a Strong Heart:
Questions and Answers from
a Consensual Slave

*Taken from the blog "Serving as
Nature Intended"*

By

Kate Ashland

Heron's Wing

**Heron's Wing Press/Heron's Wing Talon
Williamsburg, VA**

Heron's Wing Press is a creative collaborative of small press authors whose mission is, "writers helping writers." If you would like more information, contact with an author, or reproduction information please go to www.heronswing.com

This book does contain graphic sexual descriptions and adult content. It has been published for adult readers only. All activities described are for adults who are consenting to the dynamic.

"What does it take to be a consensual slave?
Soft words and a strong heart."

~kate

The Master's Permission

When my friend Ernst announced at our poker game three years ago that he was moving we were devastated. We would miss our friend, but we were crushed at the thought of losing kate. All of us are Dominant men and enjoy our submissives and consensual slaves privately and as subs at the game. But kate is the kind of slave who makes everything work. She is wicked smart, cheerful, sophisticated, obedient, sexual and energetic. She also has the calm of the deep ocean in her. We couldn't imagine the event without kate. Then, a miracle. Ernst pulled me aside after the game and said something unbelievable. "I want you to own kate."

I accepted immediately, but before my first training session with Ernst and kate I grew nervous. I've had a number of submissives and a slave before, with my wife's acceptance, but no one like kate. In fact, the one slave I owned was a disaster and nearly damaged my marriage. How was I going to own this powerhouse of a woman? I'd been served by her body, of course, like all the Masters at the game. I couldn't imagine what it was like to own her.

She was already at Ernst's when I arrived for the first session wearing her collar, cuffs, and chastity belt. She served me a drink and said Ernst would be down in a moment. She knelt on the floor beside me, completely silent. Had she even been consulted? I asked her if this was okay with her. She said, "Of course it is, Sir." I told her I didn't know how she could handle this so calmly and explained I was intimidated by the idea of owning her because I thought she should be owned by someone terrific.

She got up and left the room! I was thinking about telling Ernst this wasn't a good situation and about to go when she returned with a plate of cookies for me. She knelt back in her spot. I sat there like a fool eating cookies and thinking of ways to tell her I didn't want to own her. It was all too much. Then, I felt her hand on mine. She turned my hand over, leaned in and kissed the palm of my hand. That certainly put the wind back in my sail. I felt a small, cold piece of metal press against my flesh. It was the key to her chastity belt.

"You must be someone terrific," she said. Then calmly lowered her head and waited for Ernst to arrive. And I knew – she belonged to me.

That's kate.

For almost three years she has served my wife and me as a consensual slave. She has taught us, given to us, laughed with us, and placed herself at our disposal. She suffers under my belt, and she moans serving my body. Then she thanks me. She always thanks me. She's not "the perfect slave" (and she would be the first to tell you that), but she is the perfect kate – and that's all she needs to be.

Her time schedule is crazy and she has both work and family obligations. My wife and I also keep a demanding schedule and need time for our adult children and small grandchildren as well. When kate asked my permission to create a blog so she could be more involved in the slave community and spend more time respecting other Masters and chatting with other slaves, I granted it. When she told me people were encouraging her to collect the questions and answers from her online conversations I said I wasn't surprised (although she seems genuinely shocked by the idea). A few weeks later she asked my permission to go forward with the project and add some of her thoughts to make it a book.

I thought about all the ways she excels at what she does and how grateful she is for everything around her. I thought about how my wife went from saying, "Do what you need to do and leave me out of it" to inviting kate into our bedroom and finding comfort in kate's embrace. I thought about how the men at the poker game cheered when they learned kate wasn't leaving after all. No one needs to learn how to be like kate. But, her presence has made every life I know a little happier, smarter or calmer. Hopefully she will do that for you too.

As the owner of kate by her own consent and the man entitled to her body, mind, time and decisions – I hereby grant my permission for her to collect, write, speak and share her thoughts and experiences in this book. I hope you will value and enjoy my slave as much as I do. On behalf of my wife and myself, we give her our blessing.

Master Daniel and Lady Gaye

Foreward

The Slave Speaks
*I have always been under the authority of my lover.
I spent seven years as a spanked or dominated girlfriend,
eight years as a submissive owned by my Master/husband,
a year as an Odalisque, then after my divorce I spent four
years as a consensual slave to a Master who moved out of
state and now I am soon entering my third year with
Master Daniel. In short, I have served men over half my
life. So, with all that water under the bridge, it's no wonder
I get a lot of questions about slave life.*

*To me, the answers to almost all questions about
consensual slavery, BDSM, or relationships begin and end
at the same place. There is one answer above all others.
That one thing?*

Gratitude
*To be a consensual slave owned by a Master is about living
in gratitude. A slave is:*

- *Grateful she has someone to serve.*
- *Grateful she has the ability to serve.*
- *Grateful for training that molds and shapes her.*
- *Grateful for discipline that guides and teaches her.*
- *Grateful for sexual service to give pleasure to her Master.*
- *Grateful for domestic service to nurture and show care for her Master.*
- *Grateful for everything she is given.*
- *Grateful for everything she has been denied.*
- *Grateful for the free men and free women to be above her.*
- *Grateful for other slaves and subs, to share the journey.*
- *Grateful for good times, bad times, busy times, and quiet times.*

- *A slave is always grateful.*

In terms of this collection of questions, answers, thoughts, jokes and experience I have many to thank.

I am thankful to my Master and his wife for allowing me to speak freely and openly about them and about myself – their property.

I am thankful to my dear sister servants (and my brother servants too), Masters and free men and women who continually encouraged me to gather the questions and create this work. I would have never done it without their reinforcement.

I'm thankful for all the trailblazers who wrote about BDSM before it was trivialized by the grocery store paperbacks of romanticized fan fiction. I'm thankful to Pauline Reage because The Story of O gave me an early and clear picture of exactly how I wanted to live and who I was meant to be.

I'm thankful to everyone who asked me a question – no matter how sincere or lecherous, angry, interesting, sad or joyous.
Gratitude,
kate

Consensual Slavery, Submission & Service

The Slave Speaks

Consensual slavery. What is this all about? What are the differences between slaves and submissives? You aren't really enslaved, are you? What if your Master wants you to do something you don't approve of or do not like? Can you refuse? Do you have limits? Does your Master honor them? You can walk away any time you want, so you really aren't a slave, are you? These are the kind of questions I get when I talk about being a consensual slave.

In an environment like BDSM, a world that is literally creating and re-creating itself every day, there aren't any real "rules" or structures to help us define and understand the concepts around us. When a label carries a heavy and serious word like "slavery" it is important to ask those questions. I have asked them of myself, and am happy when someone considering the life of a consensual slave asks them as well.

Consensual slavery is the act of indenturing yourself as a piece of property to an owner. You belong to the Master. You fall into the same category as his car, his home or his pet. You are owned by him. He does what he wants to do with you. You do what he tells you and then thank him for allowing you to do it. His pleasure is your pleasure. His will is your desire. Your body is not yours. Your decisions are not yours. You will give him everything when you give your one and only power – consent.

Consent is the tool you use to help you establish limits. A slave's limits are far broader than a submissive or a daddy's girl. Once the contract is made and consent is given, the slave makes no more decisions other than how to best please her Master in all she does.

I was a submissive for a long time but always had elements of consensual slavery in my practice. As a submissive wife, I served my husband in every way and gave him all power and responsibility over my life and our belongings. After our marriage ended I took some time to research and discovered the world of consensual slavery. It was what I had been trying to achieve all along – the total all-in proposition of being owned by another person. The collar around my neck isn't just a symbol of my devotion. As a consensual slave, it is a title – a deed – and a bill of property. It isn't my "kink" – it is my identity.

Consensual slavery involves many of the same practices you find in other forms of BDSM. There is spanking, whipping, discipline and punishment, training, teasing, sexual service, domestic service, and protocol. What makes consensual slavery different is the way the slave sees herself in an objectified way. I am property. I am less than the Master as a being and he has the rights and entitlements to take pleasure from me any way he chooses, because he is a man and a Master. Seeing myself as a lower being allows me to live a life of gratitude and purpose. To start and end every day with the words, "Thank you" has changed my life in so many ways.

Simply put – it may be lonely at the top, but it is lovely at the bottom.

Who/what gave you an idea to be a slave? Just curious as to how you ended up in this interesting lifestyle.

———————⁓————————

Thank you for the question. My journey to slavery began when I was in college and experienced my sexual awakening. In college I did things my family would not have been proud of - had a boyfriend, had sex, drank a little, foul language, etc. I went home for Christmas break and for the first time realized how I missed the male dominance, structure and punishment of my childhood. I told my boyfriend back at school that I felt like I wanted to be spanked and held to a higher standard by him. He left me and told his friend I was a "weird girl." The friend, who was a spanko - probably since birth - made a point to get me alone one day and ended up spanking me over his knee with a flip flop (ah, college) - we then had sex and I connected pain and sex for the first time. We stayed in a relationship throughout undergrad, but went to different grad schools.

I had several spanking boyfriends in grad school and knew I didn't want anything else. Eventually I met the man who would be my first true Master and husband. He was into strict discipline and obedience. Early in our marriage the internet happened. We discovered a website called Usenet and found the Alt.Sex.Spanking newsgroup. For the first time I realized it wasn't "just us." We broadened my discipline and spanking routine to include submission, collars and sexual service.

Being a submissive (although I was more of a slave; we just didn't call it that back then) was a tremendous joy. We went through formal training together as my husband worked with an experienced Master and the two trained me.

At one point my husband wasn't able to maintain the role of a Dom very well as he was struggling with personal issues. We saw a therapist who specialized in BDSM couples and he suggested we try Code D' Odalisque (pleasure slavery) - where the slave is only used when the Master is ready - so he could take a break from day to day duties of a Master. What we discovered was that I did not respond well to the lack of spanking or whipping (but I did like the mindset of slavery and cock worship). So we started a transition into consensual slavery.

Eventually after 12 years of marriage my husband could not sustain himself or our relationship and our mutual decision was to divorce. I floundered for a while and then found my second long-term Master who was experienced in consensual slavery. I served him for 4 years but and he accepted a job in another state and moved. He gave me to Master Daniel, my current owner. Master Daniel's needs and my limited schedule work perfectly together. We trained together and I gave him my consent to ownership.

So – where I am now as a journey? I have spent:

7 years a spanked and dominated girlfriend

8 years a submissive

1 year an Odalisque / with domestic service

6 years in consensual slavery

By definition a slave does, without question, what the Master wants. Are there limits set up before or does the slave just trust the Master to not do anything out of line? Do you have any hard limits or when you give yourself to your Master, you give up being able to set limits?

———————⌒⌒————/————————

Thank you for this question. It is one of the defining queries of consensual service.

All people have limits. In fact, a woman who says she has no limits is either a fantasy only player or is very, very unhealthy.

My limits are: Nothing illegal, no kids, no animals, no scarring or permanent damage, no revelation without my expressed consent (i.e. you can't tell my boss I'm a slave), and no lover whose STD status has not been verified via testing. (Note: If someone has an STD, that isn't a deal breaker - they just have to use a condom and safety protocol). So, if a Master decides to share me - verification is his job to get and show me. A slave is valuable. Every Master should be willing to follow that broad set of limits.

In consensual slavery the only negotiation is the actual consent. Once you give consent to be someone's slave - you take anything they dish out and do everything they say. **Prior** to consent- you can discover if the Master will honor your limits (slave limits are usually practical and on legal lines). If I had a Master who said – "I am going to require you to wear a collar with the word 'slave' to work" - I would say upfront, "I can't consent to you." If I got into a slave relationship where the limits were understood and six months later a Master wanted me to do something to break them, I would withdraw consent.

In order to prohibit drama - my personal rule (applies only to me) is that my withdrawal is final. If I determine a Master cannot keep the agreement, I don't go back and try again later. Done is done. However, I have never withdrawn consent from a Master. I have had three Masters in my time as a slave. I have never had my limits violated - because I consented to men I knew well enough to trust not to violate them.

It's an important thing— a slave doesn't have to offer herself as a slave immediately. You can train with a Master, get to know a Master, work with him and discover if he is the right person before you give your consent and trust.

You wouldn't say to a person on a second date, "I trust you with my entire life and I have no limits." You shouldn't do it in M/s. People who are online saying after 20 minutes "You are my Master and I am your slave and I have no limits" are not responsible to themselves or others. The key to consensual slavery is to set the environment up front. Make the map, then hand HIM the steering wheel.

You seem really intelligent. How do you shut your brain off to mindlessly serve your Master like slaves do? I can't get out of my head long enough to shut down.

———————————～———————————

Thank you for the compliment and the interesting question. I must admit that I disagree a bit with the premise that the service a slave provides is "mindless." As a slave, whether I am making his dinner, ironing his clothes, on my knees worshipping his cock with my mouth, or bent over feeling the pain of him stretching my anus with his powerful member, I should be thinking about pleasing him at all times. I don't escape my mind to serve him – I use my mind to serve him.

There can be a lot of "downtime" in slavery – If I am kneeling waiting for him to arrive, I can think of ways to show my gratitude for him. If I am lying with my head in his lap, sucking him while he watches television, I can think of ways to lick, hum, or move to increase his pleasure – or if he just wants me holding him in my mouth, I can imagine what I might do for him later. I try to remember and catalog all of his preferences and desires. The mind doesn't hinder slavery – it makes it all the more engaged.

What do you do with yourself when you're not with your Master? I know you look after your parents and are a guardian to your nieces, but do you simply just stop being a slave? Do you communicate with him or his wife?

———————————— ～～ ————————————

Thanks for that great question. I think it goes to the heart of the whole issue of what happens when you don't live with a Master or when you serve a couple.

I never stop being a slave, any more than I stop having a small nose or a scar on my ankle. It is a part of me that never leaves. Even after my divorce when I took some time to recoup and had no Master - I was still a slave. You aren't a slave because someone owns you. In consensual slavery you are a slave and that's why someone owns you.

So, if I am at work - I do excellent work with the reality in my mind that my Master - the man who owns me - has sent me to this job and I must make him proud. If I am at home I do house chores or hang out with the kids or talk to my mom with the thought in my mind that my business is my Master's business and doing well by them is doing well by him. He doesn't have to be in the room with me to be in my head, heart and consciousness. If I am only a slave in his presence then I am not really a slave - I'm just role playing.

We communicate between service times but it is usually functional or sometimes fun. Right now I am preparing to go to his house and serve them a nice meal and experience for Valentine's Day. So his wife has sent me what wine they want and what they would like the menu to be. She sent me a new appetizer to try. I tried it at home, and told her I wasn't crazy about it. She picked a different dish. He gave me the location of a present he would like for me to pick up and hold as surprise for his wife.

She works near my office so occasionally she will text and ask if I can join her or join them for lunch. He sends me articles if he wants my opinion on it.

He is not a needy Master. I don't have to check in every day or say I'm thinking about him or write him after a service session and tell him how I felt about it (the online conventions are not for me). If he wants to know how I felt - he will ask me when I'm kneeling in front of him. He is secure. He knows if I had a joy, I would thank him at the time. If I had a concern I would tell him - so I don't have to give him some constant stream of attention or affirmation. For one thing - he doesn't need it. He knows he owns me - and neither of us have time or desire for it.

So - I go about my busy, happy life and he does too. Then every other week and sometimes in between I am lucky enough to serve him in person, not just in heart.

Could you fall in love with a man who truly
considered you his equal and be happy?

Could I love him? Sure. Could I live with him in a
long happy relationship? No. I've seen what happens in
couples where a vanilla person marries someone who is a
sub or slave or has a fetish. Invariably - infidelity happens
because our internal needs often over-ride our promises -
even the ones we mean to keep. I wouldn't want to do that
to someone.

But there is enough room in the world for all kinds
of love - so I could love him, and befriend him. But, that's
as far as it would go. If he isn't willing to be the head of
my household, the Master of my body and the controller of
my time, then I cannot give myself to him.

Consensual slavery is not about love. It is about
service, devotion (a form of love) and finding your pleasure
by pleasing your owner. It brings with it a great deal of
work and effort, but provides a wealth of security,
seduction and joy. A life owned by a man is a life with
meaning and purpose to me – I wouldn't trade that for the
world of sweet nothings and equal decision making.

My boyfriend has been showing me all these blogs to introduce me to this stuff because he likes it. I don't know what to think. Sometimes I get hot watching it and sometimes I feel really guilty. Doesn't it ever get to you that there are real women held captive by men like this? Those women in Ohio and sex trafficking and stuff? Have you seen movies about slavery? It's not a game. Don't you think playing at slavery is kinda gross in light of its horrors?

———————————————〜————————————————

Thanks so much for writing me and sharing your opinions and honest questions. They are good questions to ask. I know the BDSM world can be very overwhelming at first, and I promise you all of us involved have asked ourselves or others those very questions.

Every time I see or read an account of a woman (or man) held hostage or forced into sexual slavery/sex trafficking I feel angry, sad and sorry for what happened to them. When I read that the perpetrator had a website or was claiming to be a Dom or Master - I feel twice the anger and sadness. <u>I am opposed to rape, violence, coercion, and kidnapping in all its forms.</u>

However, what I talk about when I speak of my life (and what most people in the BDSM community are doing) has nothing to do with the pain you describe. Saying "people are abused so you shouldn't do BDSM" is like saying, "an improper gas heater burned a house down, so I won't use a blanket."

Here's the difference: I practice <u>Consensual</u> Slavery. It is a choice I made to give my Master power and rights over me. I have the ability to withdraw that consent and end the relationship at any time. If I were being abused in the relationship - I could say one word and protect myself.

So no, I don't relate what I do to those who experience the horrors of actual slavery. I have the power to give myself and the power to protect myself. I relate my experiences to the BDSM practice of Consensual Slavery with all the safeguards, rules and guidelines thereof.

There are things I find gross on Tumblr and in the world: hatred, abuse, non-consensual acts, prejudice, judgment, rudeness, needless drama or using one's experience, status, religion or authority to force your ideas upon another. Those things are gross to me. But, they are not part of my life – here or in the world.

I hope you and your boyfriend find some kinks that give you pleasure, joy and love – no matter what they may be.

You wrote about a "natural order" and I would love to have more information on that, because I feel so naturally drawn to feeling/being subservient and inferior to men but I find it hard sometimes to reconcile that and my life as an independent, smart, knowledgeable woman. Any thoughts that could help?

———————～———————

Thank you for writing. There are probably as many definitions of the "natural order" as there are people who believe in it. How it works in your mind and philosophy is entirely up to you. The basic idea behind the "natural order" is that men are designed biologically to be the leader/head of the relationship and women are designed to submit to their leadership and authority and provide them with pleasure, support and devotion. Natural order ideas have been found in the history or present day of almost every culture and religion. They are, however, entirely interpretive.

I very much understand how challenging it can be to exist in an environment seeking to develop you as an empowered, educated woman, and still feel sexually and personally like you prefer a man who is the authority over you. For me, that resolved by understanding I don't have to be uneducated, poor, uninvolved politically, or a doormat in order to respect and honor the authority of the man I consent to own me.

Women can be educated, have good minds, good jobs, political ideas, and most importantly self-care/protection – and still bow before a man and serve his desires and submit to his will. In fact, the smarter, more economically independent, physically fit and healthy, and involved in society I am – the more I have to bring to his table and lay before him. That awareness helped me exist in both worlds. I don't talk about the ideas of the natural order at work or with vanilla people, and I don't talk about my entitlements as a female when I'm with my Master.

To me – the original point of feminism was that women could be anyone they wanted to be. A consensual slave is who I want to be. I have the freedom to consent to do that. I can hope for a world where all women and men can choose their best path – whether it is in the boardroom or on your knees in a collar in the bedroom – or both.

I was wondering if, as a slave, you thought men were superior to women. And depending on your answer, do you think of yourself as inferior to men?

———————————————～——————————————

Thank you for such a lovely note. First, I need to note that the thoughts I give are strictly for me and my way of seeing the world. Every person has a unique way of looking at things. As a slave and an individual human who respects others – it is not my place to tell other people how to see the world. I can, however, describe my thought process to be placed on the table as a choice on the buffet of ideas we have to choose from.

Second, I would like to clarify what superior means to me. To me, superior means a place above, in authority, entitled to obedience, service, and reverence. It does not mean – as the misogynists say – "Men are more intelligent and women are brainless cunts." In fact, most of the intelligent misogynists here online admit their blogs are experiences in fantasy. Men and woman are equally intelligent or ignorant, educated or uneducated, rich or poor, able or challenged, etc. I celebrate men as superior to mean that they are set above me (as a woman) because that is their natural place, and they have all authority and entitlement thereof.

Now – why? I see and honor the superiority of men through both nature and nurture – i.e. natural and cultural conditioning. The natural – Men are designed to be instinctually assertive, aggressive, and in charge. A survey several years ago was conducted on ideation – how men and women idealize/fantasize their lives. When asked what they envisioned as a good legacy – the majority of women chose scenarios based on their children doing well in the world. The majority of men chose scenarios where they died either protecting their family or defending their country. Men have an instinct to shepherd, protect, lead and head the family.

Biologically it is clear within my sexual orientation (I'm heterosexual and other sexualities may see this differently), that men were designed for superiority. Man has a cock – it is a penetrative instrument designed to spear, impale and thrust, sexually hard. The man enters the woman, taking her, pushing himself into her and propelling his seed into her body. It doesn't matter whether it is orally, vaginally or anally. The cock dominates the void. Women are soft, wet, warm, open, designed to take in, be filled, to submit. A woman was made to be entered. Women were born to submit themselves to men.

Culturally, most (not all) societies have been structured around male dominance for a very long time. From early times forward men have been entitled to the leadership of their clans, tribes, cultures and people. As it has been for centuries, so it is in my world today.

Do you not consider the idea of consensual slavery an oxymoron? If you look at it in the end, you are really only bottoming to your desired partner, that you chose, agree on terms and then execute against the agreed terms. This is far from what I would call slavery in any meaningful use of the word.

—————————————————————

Thank you for this thought provoking question. I think your confusion results from only having half the definition of the word "oxymoron". You know an oxymoron is a word made by joining two opposing words. Like jumbo shrimp, or consensual and slavery. But the full definition is:

An oxymoron is a word made by two opposing words that creates an entirely new word or concept.

In other words - jumbo shrimp exist - and they are delicious in garlic butter. Consensual slavery exists - and it is delicious too (at least to me).

The two words are a yin/yang. Consent modifies slavery to change it from being forced to something I choose and want. Slavery modifies the consent to add a component that takes away my ability to choose particulars.

So - look at it this way. Flour + Water + Yeast — I don't eat flour. I do drink glasses of water and I don't chew on yeast. But, when you put those three together and add a little heat — bread!

Slavery without consent is wrong. Consent without slavery is dull. Put them together and add a little sexy heat - bliss!

You say that you are "an educated feminist" in the first line, but the last paragraph declares a celebration of "female objectification" amongst other things. Does this fit with being a feminist, or has that been driven out of you or relinquished when you became the slave you are now? I am not in any way calling into question anything you say, just seeking clarification. My respect to you.

———————————————

Thank you for allowing me to clarify this apparent contradiction. Feminism isn't the kind of person you are, but the belief system you hold in general (which explains male feminists - they aren't women, but believe in the rights of women). As a college educated woman, I wore the cloak feminist ideas for many years and went through a lot of conflict with my heart that was enslaved and my surroundings of feminism.

When I embraced my slavery I admitted that for me - a slave – the rigid "equality only" view of feminism is a myth that oppressed my identity instead of expanding it. When it dictates how a woman had to be instead of offering her the freedom to choose who to be, feminism is, as one of my favorite misogynist friends opines, "the cruelest thing of all."

So, for me as a consensual slave – I reject my own equality. For free women, those who are not slaves, feminism may be their answer. For a submissive who views herself equal and chooses to give her will to a man, feminism works well. For myself, it is a part of my reality and recognition of how the world can work but it is not my world.

I am submissive. I'm in love with a very caring Dom and it feels natural to submit to him, including in our everyday life. But as a progressive, enlightened woman I battle strong feelings of guilt toward what we are doing ("how can I want to feel and act inferior?" how can he love me and agree to do that?") Can you give me ideas on how to reconcile all this? Thank you!

Thanks for this question. Truly accepting a submissive nature when you live in a culture built on empowering you as a woman is such a rough maze to go through. But you can get through it and you'll love the challenge, and feeling that you do.

For me - the biggest help was realizing that through my education and in the workplace there were a lot of mentors, employees, scholars and popular authors telling me about the power, equality (and sometimes supremacy) and rights given to women. But - the truth is - those influences, though well meaning, also taught me - "There is only one right way to be a woman." And - that's a lie.

There is nothing unenlightened about being a slave by choice, a submissive or a servant. In fact, in Christian history the Bible talks repeatedly about being a slave of faith and the "least shall be greatest." In Eastern thought the idea is to serve one another and not just humble the self - but lose it in enlightened compassion for one another. There is nothing weak, wrong, dumb or anti-feminist about submission and service.

The "Man is the leader of women" idea is often called the "Natural Order" - I think it is called that because if it works for you - it feels natural. It feels right. You don't make it to feel that way - it just does. Despite what the ladies at Cosmo think - that's okay.

As a consensual slave - I am still well employed, educated, intelligent, empowered to use my mind and body in every way to please my Master. I'm not a dishrag, doormat or dependent.

My life and what I write about is consensual slavery. What you and your husband might be practicing is submission - that has an important difference. Submissives don't practice the "natural order" - they practice equality of genders where the sub gives her service to the Dom as a gift. She is not unequal - she is equal, willingly bending down because she chooses to do so. If the ideas of natural order challenge you - don't practice them. Practice submission, and give your body to the one you find worthy.

I don't understand the different types of serving men. I'm a sub (started as a little) and my Master is training me for slavery. I struggle with my attitude! How do you get over a "don't wanna do it" attitude? I usually grit my teeth and try to avoid punishment but I know I should be trying to change my mindset. Any help would be appreciated!

———————— ~ ————————

Hello Sister Servant, thanks for your note. First, I want to suggest you be a little gentle with yourself. You are attempting something extremely difficult. Little to sub to slave is not - bread to toast to stuffing. It's more like fish to cat to bird. Those three types of service are entirely different and will require a lot of time, self-knowledge, and evolution.

No type of service is better or worse than any other. There are different types of service for different types of people. Littles, subs and slaves have different personalities, histories and primary wiring. People are who they are. It is possible you are a submissive and not a slave - as such - any attempt to "change your attitude" will leave you frustrated. I went from dominated girlfriend, to sub, to odalisque, to slave. The reality is - I was always a slave — and even when I was just a girlfriend who got spanked and gave glorious blowjobs - I wanted to serve and I had the attitude we recognize as a slave attitude.

So, if your Master is willing to have a listening session - you may want to ask him to slow down, and train you to discover who you are and to be the best at that you can be. It's better for you both in the long run - because if you truly are a little who is attempting to be a slave even though it is not in your heart - it's going to feel like pretending, and that will get old.

Now - different roles in service can do the same things - littles can be anally submissive and slaves can cry big tears and want hugs. The difference isn't <u>what </u>you do — it's the motivation - **why** - you do it.

A little believes she is small, in need of leadership and protection. She wants to please her Daddy. She is punished because she is naughty (or was bratting to get punished because she and her Dom like the fun/attention.) Only her Daddy has control of her.

A submissive believes she is equal. She chooses to gift her Dom with accepting his leadership and protection. She wants to honor and trust her Dom. She is punished to correct wrongs, for erotic reasons, and for teaching. Only her Dom has control of her.

A consensual slave believes she is unequal. She was born to serve and consents to a Master/Owner, benefiting from his leadership and protection. She wants to obey and serve her Master. She is punished for any reason or no reason. She can be whipped just because she is a slave if it pleases him. Her Master has control of her but all non-slaves are above her and are entitled to respect.

See - different motivations equals different outcomes. Start with a journal or discussion that identifies what your motivation really is - and then be that person. There is nothing a slave does that a sub cannot do. If you are a submissive in your heart - be the best you can and you won't need to be a slave. If you have a slave heart - I think you'd know it.

How long were you an Odalisque? What did you
think of it? It sounds like a potentially nice
lifestyle if one is not too big on working and one I
wouldn't mind now if it could be arranged.

———————————————⌇———————————————

Thank you for your questions. I was an odalisque
for a little over a year, with three months training prior to
that. Like all submissive choices - Odalisque has plusses
and minuses. I did work during my time as an odalisque, as
my salary was supporting us and I was not willing to
abandon my career. But, I had a 9 to 5 job so the hours
were steady and allowed me to perform my other duties
well. Most modern women squeeze the life of an odalisque
into a life with a job, family, and responsibilities. It's
probably healthier than sitting around all day waiting to be
called for sex.

On the plus side - for me - I learned a tremendous
amount about the aesthetics of pleasing a man. You know
those people who laugh about having to dress up to go to
the grocery store? Well, as an odalisque you have to dress
up to go to the kitchen. Heels, hair, makeup, nails, always
must be pleasing and right. No stomping to the door in your
PJ's to let the cat out - when you leave your quarters - you
look the part at all times - 3:00 PM or 3:00 AM (you may
wear a robe, but your hair is up and you look nice). I
learned to pour coffee and tea in front of the Master, not
hiding in the kitchen. I learned to walk gracefully so no one
could hear me, so that when I serve, move or kneel I do not
disturb or distract the Master. If you are an odalisque
everything is ritual and it means living your life like a
dance. I enjoyed the large amount of private time in my
quarters and what an amazing feeling when he would call
me out to serve him.

On the minus side - for me - There were no spankings, whippings or disciplinary types of fun. Odalisque is a great way to live for a sub who doesn't have a spanking fetish. I missed the belt. I also ended up adding a lot more domestic service because someone has to do it - the laundry will not fold itself nor will the dinner magically appear. In the end, we gave Odalisque a year, then decided slavery was a better option.

The code is strict. The life is beautiful. It is much harder than the life of a general house slave. Still, I did manage to carry the soft language and voice, the graceful movements and quiet demeanor into my future service.

So submissives and slaves are different. But a Kajira and a slave are the same thing, right? I'm just trying to figure who to be and it's all kinda confusing.

———————————————

Thank you for your question. It is a little confusing sometimes. A kajira and a slave are NOT the same thing, although they share many attributes. A kajira is a Gorean slave, which means she practices the Gorean lifestyle. Gorean slavery (a lifestyle created by a series of science fiction books) is rich with ritual, methods and meaning. You can't just pop up and say "I'm a kajira." There are specific positions, veils, dances, and responses to go with being a kajira. If you are interested in Gorean life - go on forums where you can learn more about the Gor books, and meet other kajira who can prepare you for a Gorean Master who will train you.

Simply: All kajiras are slaves, but not all slaves are kajira. That is a special and honorable distinction to make. I have great respect for my kajira sisters, because there is just so much to know and remember!

I must tell you I think you may be going about this all wrong. Submission/slavery/etc. isn't something you pick off a website like a book from a shelf. Don't look at descriptions or websites and say, "I wanna be that." Look at your sexual desires, preferences and habits. Do you want to have more control over your submission and who you submit to? Is someone's pleasure more important to you than your own? Do you want a structured community to find a role in? Those kinds of questions will lead you to the best life for you.

If you are thinking of doing this in real life - don't just be a role. Be the person that you are. If this is just an internet fantasy thing — then learn about each type before making a choice and realize that you need to be upfront that you don't really intend to do these things in person. You don't want to disappoint a Master who believes you will someday sexually serve him. Most importantly – be honest with yourself.

With your belief in male supremacy what is your opinion on men who submit to women or serve as male slaves of a Mistress or a lesbian slave who is owned by a female Mistress?

Thank you for this question and a chance to talk about one of the things that's just as important to the BDSM community as safe/sane/consensual - and that is not judging others.

My opinion of anyone who lowers themselves to serve another person is high respect. It takes courage and strength to choose to bow before another and offer them something as personal as sexuality and personal service.

There is more than one way to be. Male supremacy (sometimes called the "natural order") is a guiding factor in my life. There are many other ways to see the world - all of them valid and beautiful. If female supremacy, or gender equality (most submissives view the world gender equal and their submission as a gift, most slaves view the world in some way unequal with them on the lower end of the scale) is the view that guides another person - that's great.

The key is to know who you are, and serve someone trustworthy and desirable to receive that gift. The more we listen and respect the individuality of others, the healthier our community will be.

Do you acknowledge female Dommes as superior to you? Do you feel Dommes are superior to male submissives? Thank you for your honest answers!

─────────────────────── ～ ───────────────────────

Thank you for the interesting question and chance to answer. If you look at an early Roman slave market there are three types of people - free men/women, enslaved men/women and debtors (free people enslaved only until their debt is paid). It's easy to see who is superior without regard to gender. Free people are superior to everyone, debtors are superior to slaves, and slaves are inferior to all.

Much in the same way, I view a Domme as a free woman and naturally superior to me, her gender notwithstanding. I see her superior to any slave. Dommes have a high level of both responsibility, and accountability for their slaves and deserve all honor.

I have never served a Domme, but have been at events where Dommes were served by their slaves or subs. What I observed was that when you're underneath the table pleasuring your owner as all the Doms and Dommes enjoy their conversation - the person beside you is a fellow servant and gender doesn't matter.

Just because something isn't my reality doesn't mean it isn't a reality. It is not my place as a slave to tell anyone else who they should or shouldn't be. Submissives have more leeway in choice - but slaves don't spend loads of time thinking about who is and who isn't superior to them. We spend our time trying to please those who enter into our sphere and maintain our service.

How do you feel about "it," kate? I see a lot of reference to subs/slaves as "it" rather than him, her, he, she, etc. Has anyone ever referred to you as an "it?" How did it make you feel, or if not, how would it make you feel?

———————————— ~———/————————————

      Thank you for asking me this interesting question on the issue of objectification. I have not been called "it" by anyone in real life, nor do any Masters in my group of friends do that to their subs/slaves. I have been called "it" or asked to refer to myself in the 3rd person ("this slave" and in "this slave would like to ask you a question") by men who have written me online or are online Doms. That doesn't make me feel any particular way. It is their need/comfort and doesn't affect me as a real person. I do it because it is the polite thing to do.

      How would I feel if my Master started calling me "it?" I wouldn't respond well in the long run. The word "it" not only removes status – it removes gender – and I love being a woman. My slavery is grounded, in part, in celebrating the fact that being a woman is one of the reasons I was born to serve men's sexual and personal pleasure. My Master enjoys my femininity roughly, repeatedly and with great passion. He wouldn't feel that way whipping or having sex with a genderless box. So – "it" wouldn't enhance our relationship in any way.

      "It" is used a lot by misogynists whose sexual expression is not only based on dominating women – but the hatred/reduction of women (I find most of their behavior is enacted in fantasy or online). There is a big difference in being a dominant partner and being a misogynist. Most Doms love women and want to guide, challenge and enjoy them, not objectify and discard them.

There are also a number of women who love to be completely objectified (have their humanity removed) and they get an erotic charge by being called "it." So there is definitely a community for the word that enjoys and thrives with the practice and that's good for them. The best part is that there is room in the world for all of us.

What is "formal training"?

Thank you so much for asking. Formal training is the period - usually at the beginning of a sub or slave service - when high protocol is in place and all the rules, phrases, and patterns are set for the relationship. After a set time the Master usually softens or makes changes - but in the very beginning it is good to have very strict rules/roles/punishments in order to help the slave (or sub) slip into the proper headspace and habits.

For example: If you want your slave to drop to her knees at a finger snap and open her mouth, or lower her head - you practice it over and over and over until it becomes a reflex. Good service to a Dom is instinctual and training is where the servant develops instinct. It is also a time for listening, so the Master can hear what the slave needs and learn her patterns as well.

Training is a high protocol time. The slave is kept naked in a training collar (the real collar usually bestowed after training is complete), kneeling and learning how to serve the Master whenever possible. In my original training, for 3 months I could only say one of three phrases: "Please, Sir," "Yes, Sir," and "Thank you, Sir." Any deviation without permission would result in a punishment spanking. Pretty much *anything* can bring a punishment spanking during training (much different than an erotic).

By the time the training is over - even when working in the world or spending a night out with vanilla friends at a fancy dinner – you think and understand yourself as your Master's sub or slave.

Could you describe the different kinds of training you have received? When you were married, how did the training Dom train both you and your Master husband?

———————————⟨~⟩———————————

Thank you for your clear questions and giving me the opportunity to talk about one of my most heartfelt things - the importance of training for both a slave/sub and a Master.

The first formal training I had was after my husband and I married. We were inspired by the *Story of O* and *the Sleeping Beauty Trilogy* but we felt silly. We had both just gotten doctorates but were living scenarios in those books and having long discussions about why we couldn't just "grow up." We met a guy online (on the very old Usenet forums, which used to be all there was) who was a training Dom. He spent almost six months showing us the language of BDSM, teaching us it wasn't a game and that there wasn't anything wrong with us - it was a lifestyle many were drawn toward, etc. He taught us safety mechanisms and how to live in a natural way. I was raised with parents who practiced "the natural order" but my husband was struggling with the idea of it so the training Dom helped a lot.

For me: He taught me how to be more sexually expressive, how to increase my sexual prowess and pain tolerance (kegels, lots of kegels, skin care & lots of water), how to reflect my attitude in public and private. We did a lot of work on stretching my abilities (serving them both at once, etc.). He helped me deal with the fact I made almost three times what my husband's salary was and still be submissive, etc. He was very wise about the philosophy of BDSM.

For my husband: He taught him that sometimes I needed a Master and sometimes I needed a husband. He showed my husband how to manage both roles, use different implements and the difference between sting, thud and cut (I was the teaching subject). He showed us creative things to do, how to stretch limits safely, when to enforce high protocol and when to drop it. Most importantly for my husband who had grown up in a very liberal family – he learned how to be comfortable as the Dom of his wife and that it didn't make him a pig or bad person.

As an Odalisque - a couple that had been living in a polyamorous family with several odalisques had struck out on their own and knew the therapist my husband and I saw when he was too tired/depressed/distracted to be an active Dom. They were very sweet and funny.

For me: A lot of grace lessons. How to walk quietly, how to serve food/coffee/dessert/anything, how to bathe and groom my husband in a ritual way, hair, makeup, how to get ready quickly, how to enter and leave a room properly (without creating distraction), how to deal with the downtime, and some more sexual pleasure techniques (less kegels, more tongue techniques, reiki, sensual massage).

For him: Mostly he learned how to own a pleasure slave, things to ask for, ways to include me in his day that didn't take energy from him, things to remember about how I feel as a being used only for pleasure.

For my second Master - I was divorced and out of service for a year, moved and had a new job, new life, etc. So a lot of his training (6 weeks) was refresher stuff - protocol - how he wanted me to present myself, how to stand, serve, and give myself to him. He liked to use anal hooks a lot so he taught me about accommodating those in my body. He liked rope bondage (I don't) and he taught me ways to endure it and get positive things from it. He showed me hand signals he used, how to act at the poker game (that's how I got into that group of friends), how to serve others and what he expected from that, etc.

When my second Master transferred me to my current Master it was more ritual than anything. The first training session my former Master took off my collar and had my current Master put a training collar on me and I gave him the key to my chastity belt.

For me: It was mostly talking about my submission, philosophy, abilities, practicing techniques he really enjoyed (more kegels! lots of thigh work - as he likes reverse cg). I focused on encouraging him, learning his hand signals, desires, non-verbals.

For him: it was a great experience. I'm not very verbal so my former Master taught him how to tell by my body language when I'm wearing out, if I'm in too much pain, if my back bends a certain way what it means, how to stimulate my desire and tell when I'm on the edge.

No matter how much experience a Dom or sub has - training together is so amazingly helpful - it gives you a good "manual" for non-verbals (so important), teaches you how to discuss what things really mean, provides learning in a safe environment and it's fun. Plus - if you train with an experienced couple or Dom - it helps you make friends in the community. Safe, sane, positive friendships are a good thing.

Since you don't use a safe word, your Master has to "read" you extremely well - that's part of his training, isn't it? How do you manage pain during the few hours after your whipping when you are still with him? Since he enjoys your suffering that probably helps. Would you be as sweet as you are without physical discipline, sexual denial and unquestioning obedience? Love you!

Thank you for such love and affirmation. That makes my evening great. I truly appreciate your good thoughts.

Training - my previous Master did training (2 talk sessions and 6 physical sessions) with my current Master and myself together. Then my current Master did another few weeks of training with me alone - although I was already his property by then.

What did I have to learn? My current Master's preferences - every Master is different and has different expectations and signals. For example, for oral service my former Master used to snap his fingers for me to drop to my knees, then I would ask for permission to take him in my mouth, and I would unzip his pants and take him in from the head first. My current Master does a gesture with his hand in a downward fashion and prefers I bow my head. He undoes his own zipper, I open my mouth and silently start at the base and lick up his shaft, then take him full in. He doesn't like unnecessary talking. With every Master there are procedural differences.

His learning: You are correct. I am not overly verbal, unless asked, so my former Master would whip me and point out how I acted during pain I am enjoying, pain that is pushing me, pain near my threshold and pain past my threshold. He taught my current Master ways to phrase things to help me communicate. For example: If he asks, "Do I need to stop?" I will almost always say, "No, Master" because I don't want to leave his presence. But, if he asks "Stop, rest, change or keep going," I can say "rest" or "change" and it will show if I need a break or I need to do something different.

Pain directly after a whipping: I show my pain - breathe heavily, close my eyes and center myself in front of him, make sounds that reflect my pain or my relief it's over - he loves to watch me overcome pain and work or serve him. He grows aroused when I am struggling to catch my breath and when I finally can speak/breathe the first words I gurgle are, "Thank you."

Would I be as sweet? What a beautiful question - thank you. I don't know the answer. I know my Master's discipline, sexual denial and requirement of obedience make me a better person, boss, sister and friend.

No matter where I am, how I'm dressed or what I do - I am a reflection of the man who owns me. He has told me to always hold myself to a standard that would make him proud and show him in a good light. Thus, my obedience to him encourages me to do well, be polite, care for myself and honor others. In return - I have a life I'm happy with, proud of, and grateful for. So - his control and power over my life definitely makes me a big part of who I am today.

I really like your blog because I'm just learning all this stuff. You talk a lot about training. What is different about training and any other time? What if it's not just the little who needs training? My Daddy is new too.

Thank you so much for writing and asking me these questions. I hope you enjoy learning more about yourself and your Daddy as you take this journey together. Training is something I highly believe in. It helps people establish communication patterns, gets you used to each other and can be both challenging and fun.

Since your Daddy is new, I suggest you two find a training Dom - specifically someone who is a Daddy and has a healthy relationship with his little - who can work with you two and teach you some of the best practices and ways to do things.

I have never been a little - but for a sub or slave training is different from other times in the following ways (and some of these might apply to you as well):

1. Training has a beginning and end date and specific goals - just being oriented on a new job.

2. The protocol (how you speak and act) is higher - You say "Thank you, Sir" for everything. You address and answer everything properly. You only speak when spoken to, etc. You must always be graceful, courteous and follow whatever physical commands he has for you. This teaches you how to control your words and body. You would probably say, "Thank you, Daddy."

3. Learning nonverbal cues. Gestures are a way my Master can communicate to me without speaking. Training is where I learned what all that means. By serving with

intention, I can know him and his desires without having to be told.

4. Training is a chance for him to teach what he wants and you to show what you are good at in a learning environment. There is more listening in training. There is also more punishment. Every mistake brings correction so there is a lot more spanking. After training, spanking is usually more for fun or quick punishment if you aren't being a good girl.

I'm sorry I'm not able to be more specific about DD/lg - but there are many experienced Daddies here who would probably be willing to tell your Daddy some of the things you need to know or work on. Best of luck to you and your Daddy as you learn more about this great life.

It must be hard to maintain consensual slavery in real life. Are you really as polite everyday as you are online?

———————————⁓———————————

       Thank you for your question. I am not different online than I am in real life. There is only one me - not a fantasy me and real me.

       I believe manners still matter, and was raised in such a way that poor or rude speech resulted in getting your mouth washed out with soap, at the very least. So, I'm not this way as part of my slavery as much as I'm just this way. Real life isn't different than slavery – it is part of it.

       However, I do believe a slave's speech should be as soft and pleasing as her body to all she encounters whenever possible.

How would you feel if your daughter wanted to be a slave? How would you react? Would you support her?

Thank you for this thought provoking question. I don't have a daughter but I am raising my younger sister's children. If one or both (twins) of them said they wanted to be a slave - I think I would have a time for listening, a time for teaching and then would support them.

Listening would be asking questions like:

- What do you think it means to be a slave?
- What have you done to prepare yourself?
- Do you have a plan about disease prevention and birth control?
- Do you have an understanding about the difference between BDSM and abuse?
- Do you understand consent and do you have a way out when you are no longer ready to give it?
- What do you plan to bring to a Master or Mistress?
- What do you desire for your owner to bring to you?

Teaching would be about:

- Finishing college and having career plans because you are more free to give yourself in slavery when you don't worry about who is going to support you financially and personally.
- Understanding physical health and safety needs, and mentally healthy ideas.
- Balancing yourself between worlds.

- Having people in your life you can be honest with about experiences, success and failures in BDSM and to be honest with any Master or Mistress you serve.
- Learning not to judge others. You meet a lot of different people in BDSM - Submissive men, Dominant women, and people of all sexual orientations, gender identities, economic and educational backgrounds. It is important you learn to judge actions (as safe or unsafe/healthy or unhealthy) but never people.
- Making sure you know that no matter what has happened - you can always call me and I will be there, loving you.

kate, my mum knows that I am a sub, but she sees it as a really awful and degrading thing that I do. I've tried to explain the beauty in my submission to her, but she still is stuck seeing it as bizarre and gross, and doesn't understand why I like to get hit, for example. Do you have any ideas on how to explain what submission is truly about? How can I show its beauty and meaningfulness? It's obviously not about getting hit and fucked. Thanks, darling!

———————————∽——————————

Thanks so much for your great question. I have to give a lot of honor and respect to you and your mum for talking about this. Most people don't have such open conversations with parents and it's beautiful you two can talk about this - even if you disagree.

Submission is definitely not "about getting hit and fucked." - You can do that without submission. Submission - at its most distilled component is about trust. It makes trust the center of the relationship.

Remember when your mum gave you the car keys for the first time, or the first night she left you at home without a nanny or babysitter - or just any sign of trust. You felt amazing, and she felt proud to have a daughter she could trust. Submission creates that in a relationship. You are saying to the Dom - "I give you everything - my will, my body, and my abilities - because I trust you with them." Your Dom feels elated and loved to be trusted that way and you feel proud to be able to trust that much.

All the rest of it - the language, the spanking, the sex - are just a means to create an arena for that trust to flourish.

Your mum is never going to like the idea of you being hit. It's against her nature/programming. She's your parent. She spent a lifetime trying to keep you from getting hurt. So - don't spend a lot of time on that. Explain that you may be hurt but not harmed, and that it is a sensation you enjoy. If your mum doesn't get it - that's okay. We don't have to get everything about a person to love them.

That's the bottom line in the conversation - whether she ever understands or not - she loves you. As long as you have that - all the rest is workable.

As a sub, I would like to learn how to feel less entitled, sexually of course (I always feel like pouting or sulking if I don't come when we have sex) and also in my relation to him in general. Any ideas on how to proceed?

Thanks so much for this fantastic question. Entitlement is something that impacts all of us in society in so many ways. The most peaceful and wise people I know work to heal it.

Remember that sex starts, proceeds and ends not only in the brain, but also in the mind. Your brain is a machine that uses impulses and signals to release chemicals at certain times to create arousal, muscle tightening, muscle release/orgasm, feelings of pleasure. Your mind - your mental cognition - is the key to the impulses your brain gets. Your attitude about something actually tells your brain how to interpret the signals.

For example: Let's say your Dom wants oral service and he's sleepy so you know afterward he's going to lean back in his chair and nod off leaving you without climax. If you think, "Damn, I'm gonna do all this work to give him a blow job and get nothing. This is the worst." Your brain isn't going to release dopamine (pleasure chemical) because the mind has said, "Wait. No. This isn't good." But - if you think, "I am getting a chance to bring him into my body to nurture and pleasure him. When he wakes up he'll know how much I care for him and I'm so lucky to get to show that." Your brain is going to release dopamine because the mind says "Hey, this is a good thing."

TLDR: Gratitude is good for your sex life.

Make a decision to live your life with a sense of gratitude. Instead of thinking, "I didn't get to come." - stop. Wait. Change it to, "I got to be with my Dom. I got to submit." Tell him that you are going to spend a certain amount of time cultivating a grateful attitude - encourage him to be aware of that and be responsive to you.

When you think about it - (or watch the news) you learn that simply being alive is a gift of the Universe - along with food, shelter, someone to love, etc. There is so much we have - every moment of the day. Also, read some blogs by sister subs in the community - remember a time you didn't have someone to serve or just listen to the words of a sub craving a Master. Your opportunities to serve will seem like winning a lottery. All of us have much to be grateful for.

You blog like a perfect woman. How do you go about dating to find like-minded folks? How "out" are you about your slave status in your community? How do you balance that?

———————————⌇———————————

Thank you for this lovely compliment. I am FAR from perfect and strive every day to learn, share and grow in my slavery and personal development. I don't suppose there really are perfect people - that's what makes us all interesting.

I have a Master and have not dated for a very long time. I have a group of friends, made over time/munches/conventions, who are similar to me in job status, background and age. We gather together for private parties, poker games, sharing and service. That was where I met my Master. I think the best way to meet someone like-minded in real life is be a part of your local community and encourage others in their quest for service and freedom through BDSM.

In public I am very private about the fact I am a slave. I have a high profile job and a social and family reputation to maintain. In my group of friends, with my Master and his wife, and with my sisters I am open. I balance it by being very polite, professional and detached at work, and being open, serving and grateful with friends. I am **always** a slave - I just don't always look like one to the casual observer.

My Master and I love each other very dearly and we are willing to engage in some form of Total Power Exchange (TPE). I am still new to the lifestyle, although I've felt submissive all my life. I need to read about different people's experiences of TPE. I need answers, and questions. I'm only looking for sane, healthy testimonies. Know where I could turn to?

———————————— ～ ————————————

Thanks for this fantastic question. The key to the answer is in the two words you use: sane and healthy.

The best way to make TPE work for you is to design it together to fit your life, your gifts, and your limitations. No two couples look the same - but there are many who have TPE in their marriage. The best way is to meet people in the kink community (in person if possible, online if not) who are doing so and see how it works for them. Watch out for online testimonies - there is a lot of "head play" and numerous "fantasy" ideas out there by those who don't really live this life. You'll see these "A Dom Should Always…" or "Protocol for a Sub"…lists and they are profound, sweet or sexy - but not realistic in any way. Avoid that stuff and go with real people with real joys and real challenges.

How to tell what's sane and healthy? Here's my benchmarks:

1. **Is it possible?** Avoid the "A sub must be kneeling 24/7 naked" or "she must wear a plug to work every day" stuff - that's not feasible in any real life.

2. **Is it legal, reasonable, and medically appropriate?** Avoid the "I'm gonna keep you in a cage and feed you nothing but cum for a weekend" crap. You

should also avoid things that involve sex without protection from STD's, feces-related diseases, permanent damage, etc.

3. **Does it change and grow?** Healthy things change and grow over time. If it is very rigid or unchanging, it's unhealthy.

4. **Does if offer input, evaluation and re-structuring?** No one thing works for everyone forever. If there is nothing in your TPE that allows the arrangement to be discussed in terms of what is working, what isn't, what needs to change — then it's a cage, not a life.

5. **Is it flexible enough to accommodate needs?** TPE is a great thing, but you also need to be able to say, "I have a work deadline. I can't worship your cock right now." You both need to be able to say, "I've worked all day, I'm tired and I don't have the energy for a spanking. Let's watch some TV." Sometimes your in-laws drop in. Sometimes you have to work overtime. Sometimes you had too much spicy Italian sausage and you feel like if you have to bend over and take him you'll toss your dinner right on the bedspread - so you have to say, "I'm sorry. I can't right now." Real TPE means real exceptions.

6. **Is it natural?** Playing a role is fine for an afternoon session at a hotel, but you can't live while play acting. Does the idea and its presentation come out of you naturally or do you feel like you are presenting a front?

7. **Does it make your life better?** A healthy situation issues in goodness to all around. If TPE isn't making your life and love better - it needs to be re-evaluated and changed in structure. TPE is a choice, and a joy — if it is draining you more than giving to you - it's not doing its job.

Hope that will help guide you to filter the things you see, read, and people you know so that you can make the best life and love for both of you.

You mentioned that your older sister knows about your lifestyle. How did you tell her (or did she guess)? I can't imagine telling my sister about my sex life--she'd be totally freaked out and (worst of all) would tell everyone about her freaky kinky sister! I envy the trust and bond you have with your sister.

Thank you for this wonderful question. I think every set of sisters has a unique relationship made of childhood experiences, adult realities and personalities. I've never met any two sister relationships that were actually alike.

Growing up, my sisters and I really needed each other. Farm life is hard and our parents were strict - so we always relied on each other to keep secrets, cover for each other, etc. But we do a lot of teasing too. One thing our family tried to teach us is not to judge one another or other people. So - my sister would never judge me about being a consensual slave any more than I would judge her for some of her decisions.

My older sister is two years older than I am so she got out of the house and into the world before me. When the time came for me to leave she was the "fount of sexual knowledge" I drew from. She met my second boyfriend (my first Dom/spanking boyfriend) and she thought he was boring and not very bright. She asked me what I saw in him and I said, "He likes weird things." And she didn't say anything. Eventually I said, "I like weird things too." She asked what and I told her I liked being tied down, spanked, and ordered around. I said it was sexual and natural feeling to me. She just shrugged and said, "Everybody likes something weird, Kate. Just be safe."

It would never be her thing - she's very vanilla —
but she doesn't judge me. She's curious sometimes. She
asks me personal things now and then. But I ask her
personal stuff too. So, it's all good.

My rule of thumb is - if you don't trust them, don't
tell them. If your sister can't be trusted not to broadcast
your "freaky kinkyness" (which sounds great to me) - then
find a friend who is a sister in heart - and trust her with
your story.

Does your sister know your Master? What is really beautiful to me is his complete trust of you. I'm assuming he is one of your men your sister definitely approves of. Is that true?

———————————⌒———————————

Thank you for this question and your lovely words and compliments. It always feels good to be affirmed and I appreciate that.

She has gone to movies, shows and a festival or two with my Master, his wife and me on occasion. She is vanilla so it was an adjustment. The very first time was a traveling Broadway company showing Beauty and the Beast. Master Daniel said to ask if she would like to join us because her spouse was out of town. I asked her and she wanted to know if she had to see me serve them. I told her I would be serving them in the usual ways - getting their wine, insuring their comfort, etc. Then she said, "But you won't be naked or blowing him while I'm there - will you?" I nearly fell out of my chair laughing and said, "No. I don't generally go naked or give blow jobs at Broadway shows." So - after that she felt comfortable to tag along at events, but no more than that. She likes my Master as a person. She doesn't approve or disapprove of my life. She just loves me.

I think many vanilla people in our lives would become more accepting if we made it clear how natural and normal our lives really are on the inside. I'm no different than any other woman in most ways. My sexuality is expressed differently, and I live with a different set of "how I do things." Different people have different ways of doing everything – washing dishes, dressing, choosing a movie. But when you get to the basics – we are all just regular people.

Explain what you mean in your bio when you say, "I may be sitting at the leader's table, but in my heart - I am ever and always aware of my consensual slavery." How do you go about doing this?

———————————⁓———————————

Thank you for the question and the chance to share some about me with you. At work I have an extremely powerful position as a department head and upper division supervisor. I have a number of people who work for me, or who need my department so their department can function. It gives me a lot of power over others, including men. However, I am always mindful that while I fulfill the duties of my office as a professional, I am - underneath that role - a slave. I do that in several ways.

1. At work, I am all business. I follow every policy and company procedure to the letter. That way - I am not lording myself over men - but simply doing my job as a slave would - following the instructions set before her. I don't bend rules, I don't over-enforce them. I just follow them.

2. I don't socialize at work. I go to work, and when I am done I leave. I don't do birthday clubs, dinners with girls (or guys) or make idle chatter with anyone. My employees find me icy, but efficient - and comforting because there are no blurred lines. I do give gifts (birthday/Christmas) to my personal assistant who is female, and that is it. I am very clear my work life and real life are different and do not intersect. This isolates me from worrying about slipping into slave-mode on the job, and keeps me from bringing the power of my job into my slavery.

3. I am always shaved and even in business meetings feel the naked skin of my sex separating me

mentally from the free women and men at the table. I may be leading a meeting, but I am bald underneath.

4. I see my Master on Fridays - by Monday I am still welted, tender or bruised and it is a good reminder to me about my true place and nature.

5 Our culture is so backwards, in terms of behavior, that respect and politeness seem odd. I always say, "Thank you," "Please," etc. to men at work and everywhere else (the mailman, the mechanic, etc.) People think I am "oddly polite" - without realizing it is a verbal form of acknowledgement of their status as free people.

Dear kate: The human impulse to serve takes many forms; I honor them all -or most of them. Women who read you will want to know how you fit together the public and private life. How do you handle that?

———————————— ～～———————————

Thank you, Sir for your question. I fit together my public and private life easily now - because I have an understanding between the internal and external. Too often slaves, particularly new or young slaves, and Masters are encouraged to deal with the "external" or outside appearance. For example - you'll see pictures all over of bracelets or necklaces that are secretly collars or remind them of their servitude. There's nothing wrong with that - but it's fleeting and external. I don't need a bracelet or a secret "club ring" to know I'm a slave. I'm a slave in my heart. It is internal. It doesn't matter if I'm naked or wearing a business suit – I'm still a slave. If a slave is caught up in all the "things" of slavery - but doesn't develop the internal reality of slavery - then it's just role-play and not very sustaining.

Rings, collars, welts - they only have power from the outside if the heart is tuned on the inside. I don't wear a collar to my office. But I do treat the men in my office with respect. I look like every other woman at the post office, yet I call the mailman, "Sir."

Slavery isn't about you. It's <u>inside</u> you. Once women embrace that - the balance and transition become natural, because slavery, above all else - is natural.

Masters and Slaves

The Slave Speaks

Having a Master doesn't make you a slave. You are a slave first. Consensual slavery starts deep in a woman's psyche. There is something inside a woman that drives her to lay down her power and entitlements. Sometimes it is a need for authority to guide her, or a passion for being of service, or just a "this is right" feeling when in situations where the Natural Order (male superiority, female submission) occurs. But make no mistake, long before you kneel and take a man's collar around your neck, you were a slave.

Once you accept your consensual slavery and give yourself to a Master as his property and personal servant, a host of joys and challenges open up before you. Master/slave is more than just a set of roles – it's a relationship. That brings all the issues any couple faces - communication, missteps, issues and questions – along with all the securities, devotion and adventurous sex couples enjoy. To be owned is to be consumed by his passion and will. That can elate and terrify you at the same time.

Many of the questions I receive deal with likes and dislikes, the responsibility of Masters and the protocols for slaves. What happens when the lines between the two are not so clear? What kinds of acts show a slave's devotion to her Master? Do you serve your Master out of love or obedience? What happens when your Master wants to share you with another man? What if you don't want to share him?

These are deep, dear emotional queries and they deserve the utmost attention and care to answer. I try very hard to share my experience and give suggestions but never tell someone what they "must" do – because no person can truly know the life of another. I do not judge what I hear, but I do listen and voice my concern when a situation goes past kink to abuse or a woman is being pressured to be something she is not.

Working through our rituals, differences, disappointments and desires is a part of daily life in relationship. One thing is for sure, though. Masters and slaves are like a lock and a key. You can have either one individually – but they are better when they fit together.

I'm a 25 year old male who wants to be a Master and have been searching for a slave for quite some time but have never been successful. Any suggestions as to where I could start looking for one?

—————————

Thank you so much for writing me. I am honored you would ask my opinion. I am not sure if you are looking for an online experience or a real life one so I will give you my thoughts on both. (in the best of worlds online becomes real life at some point as well).

1. First - start with you. Do you know what it means to Master a slave? What kind of service can you afford in terms of time, costs, and communication? What is your philosophy as a Master? Do you have a training structure in mind for a slave that is realistic and healthy? For a man to Master a woman, he must first be Master of himself. Are you in a good place in your life in which to bring a slave? A consensual slave must trust you can meet your own needs (emotionally, personally, financially) before she will make herself vulnerable to you.

2. Second - get a mentor. Even experienced Masters learn and benefit when they have other friends who are Dominants or Masters to share ideas, mentor each other and support one another in friendship. Some of the best experiences my Masters had came from talking with others or discussing techniques. A mentor may also share or involve a slave in teaching you a technique or just like to have a trusted friend to use their slave or double-end her. A mentor may also be able to introduce you to a slave looking for service who would be a good match for you.

3. Get involved in the community near you (for real time) or the community online. It is not likely you're going to meet a girl out and about in the vanilla world who just

happens to secretly want to be a consensual slave. The BDSM community has so many roles, facets, and interesting people. If your job or social status prohibits local munches, find one in a town within driving distance or join an online group of friends.

4. Meet a woman you enjoy for her personality, skills, interests and charms. As you become friends and begin to lean toward lovers - discuss her sexual evolution with her. She may be someone willing to slowly and sanely grow in submission - or she may not. If not, stay friends (it's always good to have friends) and meet someone else - and if she is open - develop your relationship. Few women come of sexual age and say BAM! I'm a slave! It's a journey. Someone walked all of us onto this road.

5. Online fetish dating sites. This is the least productive place to look if you are wanting real life people and submission but it can springboard you into the community.

My (very serious) boyfriend and I have meddled with M/s on and off for about 6 months. Ever since I was little, I know that this is something I need. I was born to serve, to please, to be used. However, I feel like my boyfriend can't really give me what I need, no matter how much I beg and express to him what I need/want. He says, "Maybe I am just not a Dominant." But this frustrates me further because I see all the signs. He is dominant! Each day it just gets harder and harder. Please help in any way you can.

———————————————

Thank you for sharing your story and concern with me. I can hear the pain and worry in your words and I truly wish it was not so. It is very hard to be free in slavery when you are weighed down by so much concern. I don't know what the next road or decision might be for you - but I can give you my perspective and suggestions.

1. You can't make someone see their own dominance, any more than someone can "make you" be a slave. It has to come from within and it has to be a desire he connects with or even the best of it is just play-acting. That may be why you don't feel like your needs are being met. He hasn't connected with a dominant core so you feel like he's acting.

2. Don't be too harsh with him about that. First, it is not in the nature of a slave to upbraid a man whom she wants to own her, and second - the fact that he is *trying* to dominate you when he doesn't yet feel it means he loves you and wants to give you fulfillment. That shows there's a good man there. Don't lose sight of that.

3. Being used and being owned are great feelings. But remember, the focus of a slave isn't about what she

wants - but what she wants to give to the Master/Dom. Instead of thinking, "You're not domineering enough for me," flip that around to say, "What can I do to further submit to you and please you?" Getting your mind off of you will ease you into being more able to enjoy being into pleasing him.

4. Try different ways of enacting your relationship. For some men (or women) 24/7 D/s or M/s is too overwhelming - particularly when it isn't the "go-to" state of being. Maybe start with weekends, or pick a time and say, "This Mon-Wed is a slave set of days," and then live your normal lives in the meantime. As he gets used to slave weekends, slave trips, slave times - they will become longer and longer and he can also have downtime.

5. Some men just don't want to be in charge all the time. They get tired, bored, they just want to watch TV or go to a movie like everyone else. Having "downtime" gives him a chance to rest (and think of new ideas) and then he can return with more passion for the event.

6. Do what you're doing well - keep being honest - keep submitting - keep encouraging. To be a slave is to live every moment you can in a state of gratitude. Be grateful for him, shower him with your desire for his body, his service, and his rough love. Maybe he will find himself in that.

My Master & I have been in a D/s 24/7 relationship for about 2-3 months now. Things are going great, he's understanding & learning more than what I could expect. However, I truly only feel the power exchange and the dynamic when he is punishing me, because then he acts like a true Dom. I get confused & sad, as this isn't what I want. Do you have any suggestions as to how we could move forward?

—————

Thank you for writing me, and honoring me with your feelings about your situation. I am sorry there has been disappointment in your transition to 24/7 submission. 24/7 submission is very different than session based or online submission. Here's my best thoughts.

In session based submission where you experience BDSM in punishment/sex/service sessions but you aren't living it every minute – there are start times, stop times, you can arrange the time, you can change the schedule and when you are doing it – everything else stops. In 24/7 you can't stop life. Along with the spanking and fun comes the laundry, the phone calls, the flu, distractions and tiredness, other friends and necessary conversations about bills, groceries and plans. For 24/7 life you have to remember that everything you do is submission – even if it is not spanking or sex. Folding the laundry is submitting, reviewing your budget is submitting, going to the grocery store and ensuring he makes the choices for your purchases (unless he has assigned that to you) is submitting. Your attitude - all the time - is submitting.

One thing that helps is submissive language. In training subs and slaves ideally learn how to use submissive language all the time. Make sure your words and attitude always reflect your status.

For example – get the everyday words like "tell, want, need, get, etc." out of your vocabulary and put in "I would like, I ask, Please, and Thank you" in as better choices. Don't say to a Master – "I want to see that TV show." But, "I would like to see that TV show," or "I ask to see that TV show." Never <u>tell</u>, always: ask, invite, or offer. So it's not, "Let's go over the bills tonight." Or "Hand me that spice over there, my hands are full." - You would say "May we go over the bills, please?" Or "If you please, will you hand me the spice?" Instead of coming in from work and saying, "I need to change into my collar." Say, "Please allow me to change into my collar." Instead of "Wait a minute while I get ready." It should be, "I ask for a few moments to get ready." Keep talking in ways that reflect your submission and his power – and you'll feel it more and more in every moment of the day as he grows into the role as well.

The other thing to remember is that being a Dom isn't just a set of actions. A Dom isn't just a spanker, lover, guide, and teacher. A Dom isn't just someone who barks orders and gives rewards. A Dom is a human being. Doms get tired, Doms get bored, Doms want to put their feet up and watch TV. As exciting as the sex and punishment is for him – there are going to be times when he just wants to sit down, shut off, and chill out. Yet, even when he's lying on the couch taking a nap with the TV on he is still your Dom. Serve him when he's napping – make him a snack for later or sit beside the couch to be there when he wakes up. Ask him if you can bring his pillow or make him comfortable. If he is out of ideas for sessions, ask him to look at some resources online or get some books with fun romantic ideas that you two can see together.

On websites like Tumblr we show thousands of sexy pictures of spanking, rough sex, sexual play and bondage. No one wants to see a picture of me putting away groceries, or typing the finances into the computer. It's dull. But that's submission too. Still, those hot spanking/sex events make life great. The best thing to do is continue to have sessions. Set aside a night of the week as a "play night" where you can engage in the fun and extremes or challenges that are exciting. It will give you something to look forward to during the week. Sex and spankings can still happen in your daily routine – but a session can bring it all together in a delicious way.

Finally, he is still learning. He is on a journey. You are too. I am too. We all continue to develop as Doms and Masters, subs and slaves. Patient progress is the best way for this to happen. If you know of an older or more experienced Dom who can work with you two as a couple through some training work – it may help your Dom settle into the role. But remember- it is not your job to turn him into the Dom you want him to be, or the trainer's role to turn him into the Dom the trainer is –best is for him to become the Dom he was made to be. That takes time, experience, and confidence. Make sure he has those things as well.

I can see you are committed to your submission, and the fact he has learned and come into this life for you shows his commitment to you. That, and that alone, makes him "true" in his intention. Don't let the ideas of what some others do or claim make you think he is not a "true Dom." If he is true in his heart, and strong and steady in his actions – he is on the right path as a Dom. Serve him with a full and gentle heart and experience that submission you desire so well.

I see a lot of things saying a Dom/me, DD, Master, should never punish their submissive, little, partner, in anger. Is this the same in consensual slavery? Has your Master ever punished you because he was angry?

———————————————⌇———————————————

     Thank you for this important question. A person of power (Dom, Master, Daddy, Mistress, etc.) should never punish or strike a person without power (sub, slave, lg, etc.) in anger or while angry.

     Striking in anger shows a loss of control. For a Master to control others he must first be in control of himself. Anger, with its energy and emotion, is not a state that encourages self-control. So, when a Master is out of control, but controlling another - the situation is abusive.

     It is the same in consensual slavery - remember the key is consent. If my Master were not in control of himself, I would not consent to him being in control of me. My Master has never punished me in anger (either from my actions or due to the actions of another) - I am his property, but my role in his life is not punching bag. It's slave. He would never violate my value to him by battering me in an angry state.

     People are human. People get angry. It's natural. Anger, like all emotions isn't bad or good - it just is what it is. However, acting out of anger or striking out in anger is wrong. There is always a better way.

In your experience (or even just in your opinion), is it possible for a Master to respect your limits and still push you "too far?" I'm a newer Dom, and worried I'll get carried away. Thanks!

———————————～——————————

What a great question, Sir. Thank you. Yes, I believe it is possible to push too hard, too far (usually the issue is too fast). But, the more conscious you are of that – the less likely you are to do it.

It is easier to avoid pushing hard limits. They are understandable and clear to see. Soft limits – those kind which are made to be pushed – are sometimes harder to around the edges. The key is to know your sub extremely well before you start pushing limits. Subs have a tendency to agree verbally, even when they disagree internally, because they want to please you. So you will need an understanding of her tone of voice, non-verbal communication, pain/discomfort signals before you start pushing her places she didn't know she was ready to go.

The other thing that helps you avoid pushing too far/hard is to clarify – in yourself and with her – why you are leading her that direction. What does pushing that limit do for you? What does pushing that limit do for her? The more a sub or slave understands there is a motivation other than, "I'm the Dom so do what I say" or "I'm pushing this because pushing limits is what Doms do" the easier to stretch and obey.

Because the "list of limits" is one of the first things we discuss in creating a new coupling, there is this tendency to jump right into "here's where I want to push you." But time is one of the best tools in the Dom's toolbox. Spend your early time getting to know her, enjoying her submission, laughing, loving, spanking, etc.

Have fun with each other. Dig deep with each other. After that, go back to the soft limit list and start guiding her through the valley of opening. She'll be more ready, and you'll be more confident.

I'm always touched by the way you credit your
Master with teaching you so much, but you were
unusually experienced and well-trained when you
met him. What have you especially valued from
your Master that enhances what you brought to
him? I'm sure it's a two-way street.

———————————————

     Thank you so much for your thoughts. It always
makes me feel good to hear affirming things. Our
community is truly a vibrant one.
     The truth in BDSM, just like in life, is that every
person and experience adds to our bank of wisdom - good
and bad - so that if we do this long enough - we sort out the
great, learn from the horrible and leave the rest behind.
Coming to this Master did give me a wealth of knowledge.
     In terms of my current Master, he has given me a
great gift in trust and learning to be a slave while in the
public world. He knew when he took ownership of me that
my time was very segmented between care of my parents,
my nieces and my job. He struck the perfect balance.
     I see so many Doms (particularly online Doms)
just hammer slaves/subs with emails - wanting them to
check in, telling them what to wear, telling them to do
things at work, asking them to touch themselves in the car
during lunch, or wanting an essay at night about something.
I have also seen other Doms who are very detached once
the session is over. Sort of a "see you next time" effect.
My Master doesn't do either of those things - he's not
needy, and he's not aloof. He expects me to handle myself
a certain way at all times- respectful, responsible, and right.
     I feel the expectation and understanding that
everything I do reflects on him, and it reminds me of my
slavery to him in delicious ways throughout the day. When
I look good, My Master looks good (whether people know

he is my Master or not), and when I succeed my Master is credited upon that success. I want him to be proud and honored. So - he was able to give me a slave mind and heart for all the time, not just when I am with him. That means more to me than any superficial series of checks and balances.

I think that he has a great gift - he sets expectations then backs off and trusts me to achieve them. He doesn't demand, he expects. It's natural and pleasurable.

I'd be interested in knowing what you find attractive in a Dom (in terms of attitudes and behaviors) and the larger question (if you're comfortable speaking to it) on what types or traits other submissives or slaves are looking for in a Master/Dom?

———————————⌢̲————————————

What I find attractive in a Master or Dom:

1. **Intelligence** - not fake "know it all" intelligence - the real kind where you put in the study or got the work experience and know what you're talking about. 2 Tips:

A. Intelligence shows without saying. A Dom who tries to tell me how smart he is — isn't.

B. One of the best things a Dom can truthfully say is, "I don't know." Intelligent people don't pretend to know everything and don't make stuff up. "Know it alls" are fakes, and annoying.

2. **Confidence** - Men who know what they have and don't, what they are good at and carry themselves with assurance are very attractive. There is a difference between confidence and arrogance. 2 Tips:

A. Confident people don't tell you how great they are. That's a mark of insecurity and arrogance.

B. Confident people don't need you to tell them how great they are. Needy behavior is highly unattractive to me.

3. **Humor** - I love a man with a good sense of humor - the kind that is quick and deep — not stupid puns, and not laughing at another person — just good solid humor. I like a certain level of sophistication in humor, not fart jokes or crude phrases.

4. **Happy** - We don't, as a society, value happiness enough. Men who are happy tend to be settled, they still have dreams and ambitions but they also are in a place

where they appreciate the good things around them and are confident and comfortable enough to enjoy it. Give me a happy guy who knows how to deal with issues in a healthy way. As a slave it's not my job to make a Master happy - happiness comes from within. It's my job to give him pleasure - that's different.

5. **Decisive but reasonable** - I like men who know what they are going to do and want. I don't care for Doms who ask "what do you want to do?" or "Do you want the belt or a paddle?" If I wanted to make decisions I wouldn't be a slave! I like Masters who say "Bend over that bed, this is what is going to happen." It is great when a Dom has a plan. But, I also enjoy some kind of sense or reason behind the decisions - even if it is just "I'm going to use the belt to redden you today because I like that sound or it gives me pleasure." Just random things that make no sense disinterest me. They make me feel like he's just throwing everything together as he goes along.

As to what other slaves or submissives want - I really can't say - every woman is different and has different needs and different desires. That's why talking to a woman before you commit to being her Dom is the best course of action.

So here's the deal: I want to be a sub but I need to find a Dom.....help please.

———————⌒∿⌒/———————

Thank you for this note. The first thing to realize is that you do not need a Dom to be a sub. Being a submissive starts inside <u>you</u> with your desire to submit to another. A Dom can train you, grow with you and amplify your desires - but the seed of submission comes from within you.

1. **First - start with you.** What does it mean to you to be a sub? What is it about submission that makes you want this life? What are your limits? What are you willing to do? Every sub has limits. Know yourself. Know yours. Submitting means putting a lot of your sexual needs to the side to serve the Dom's needs. Usually, in a strong pairing, the needs are the same. How well will you deal with the loss of self. What kind of submission are you drawn toward? Are you a "little," a regular submissive, or a pleasure sub only? Know as much about yourself and your submission as possible.

2. **Create a safety protocol.** There are a bunch of articles online that tell you how to meet a Dom safely so I won't list it all here. Bad Doms and predators are all over. If you go on any site and write "I'm a single sub looking for a Dom" - you'll get a ton of mail - but most will be abusive men, people who are not experienced or safe. A man who jumps on you in the first 10 minutes very likely doesn't have a sub for important reasons. Learn how to pace communication, how to create a safe person, safe call, etc. Create a list of what you will and will not do/say/share with a stranger and *stick to it*. Have someone who always knows where you go and who you are going to meet.

3. Second - get a Trainer. If you have not been a submissive partner before (or even if you have) training is a great way to learn the ropes without losing your first D/s relationship over inexperience or lack of communication. There are many Doms with full-time slaves or subs of their own who would be willing to take you under their wing for 3 to 6 months and train you - aware they are releasing you to submit to a Master of your own in time. Training works out the rough spots so when you meet a Dom you have a good idea of the attitude, requirements and expectations of a sub. Plus, a training Dom may also find you a Dom that is compatible to you. The other nice thing about a training situation is you meet and work with sister slaves or subs. So you create friendships as well.

4. Get involved in the community - make friends who are subs and encourage and support them as they encourage and support you. You can also share your insights with them. Every person alive has something to learn and something to teach. Sister subs can also help you find a Dom or invite you to a munch or event where you meet others. A sub may ask her Dom to train you or know of someone who would be a good match for you.

5. Go to a munch, local gathering or fetish convention. There you can be in the community and meet a lot of neat people. If you can't be seen where you live, find a town within a reasonable range of distance and go there.

3 Most important things for your journey:
1. Be safe
2. Be yourself
3. Be honest

Sir is older than me and more experienced, which is good because I can sometimes use some instructing. However, Sir is a switch. I can submit very easily, but there is no part of me that desires to be dominant over him. How do I please Him when He's feeling subby? I feel very lost.

Thank you so much for asking my opinion. I know it is a painful and difficult situation when you want to be pleasing but don't have the ability to do something required. There are some people who can turn their submission on and off like opening and closing a cabinet. Others have a submissive nature that doesn't change and can't be switched off. Your job is to know which of those you are – and be that person. You can't crawl into the skin of anyone else – it won't fit.

A Sir can teach you to learn new things.

A Sir can encourage you to stretch your experiences.

A Sir can work with you to perfect your service.

But – A Sir cannot command, change, or force you to be someone that you are not.

It just doesn't work.

Someone asked me not long ago if I was ever forced by my Master to dominate other subs for his amusement and I told that person, "No." When he asked, "Why not?" I replied that it would be useless. I am a slave – a submissive woman from beginning to end. If I tried to Dom someone it would be a comedy. I'd be like "Please, bend over. Thank you for bending over. Now, I'm going to ask you to get on your knees. Please get on your knees. Oh, thank you for listening to me."

I don't have it in me to be domineering, and commanding me to try that is just going to result in frustration for everyone. The best thing I can do for my Master is be honest about that.

The right thing to do in any situation is come from a place of honesty. Consider asking your Sir if you may speak freely, and convey to him that it is not that you don't want him to feel pleasure – but you simply are not capable of doing what he requests. As Sir and sub – you are still a team – work together to find a solution that allows him the pleasure he desires, and yet doesn't put you in a position where you have to fake something or be someone you are not.

Perhaps he would be willing to find a Domme or Master to work with you both as a couple, where you could both serve that person for a session. Perhaps he can find ways to submit to you that don't require you to be over him. Perhaps he can find another outlet for when he is "feeling subby."

A relationship that isn't based on honesty isn't going to produce the best outcome for either person. My hope is by embracing the truth about who each of you is as a being you can work together to find a path that gives you joy and pleasure.

Dear kate: It seems to me that subs speak frequently about their craving for humiliation, while slaves refer instead to their craving for objectification. Say something about this difference if you recognize it.

———————————————〜———————————————

Thank you for the interesting question. I appreciate you asking my opinion. Submissives and slaves are very different women. One isn't better or worse than the other – they are just different and a lot of people get hurt or disappointed when people use those words interchangeably.

I think the fundamental difference found in your question is how the woman sees and understands herself. Submissives tend to see themselves as equal people who are "choosing" to "give" their submission to the Man. Think of all the pictures you see with stuff like "Submission is a gift she gives to you," "Don't forget the aftercare," or "A submissive has these rights…" and so on. Because submissives see themselves as women who are equal to men, but bowing to men out of choice, the shame of humiliation is a turn on. Here she is – an equal being – doing some embarrassing thing the Master commands to show her love and submission to him even though it shames her. Shame can be a very sexy motivator.

Slaves, on the other hand, do not see themselves as equal. They don't see their obedience as a "gift" – they see it as a fact. To slaves, doing what the Master says isn't something they choose – it is a duty they have to perform. The only choice consensual slaves have is to choose to accept their slavery and live it. Slaves don't have safe words, slaves don't have many choices, and slaves don't have "aftercare." In fact, a slave is expected to take care of her needs after the Master has used her. When a Master treats a slave well, slaves have gratitude – and many Masters do choose to provide nurturing or love after usage – but it is the Master's gift to the slave (not the other way around).

It is hard to feel shame or be humiliated as a slave. Because you aren't choosing the acts – you are following orders. Being objectified is a turn on for slaves because they are being used – like a tool – and meeting the Master's pleasure. Turning a slave into a laptop table means she is giving the Master pleasure as an object that is helpful – and that is what a slave is geared to always do – give pleasure and be useful.

In real terms it looks like this. A Master tells both a submissive and a slave to put a dildo in her ass and write "whore" across her cheeks, post a picture. When a submissive does it she thinks, "Wow, how embarrassing." When a slave she thinks, "The Master chose to display my ass. I must obey him."

Same act; different ideas.

About the always naked when possible thing: it's not *just* about sex, is it? Yours is not a life of constant fucking. So it must be something like the strong sign of total availability, yes?

───────────────◇───────────────

Nudity is definitely not about sex - but about the awareness of self and the display of property. A slave has no privacy and clothing can make you expect it (especially a new slave). Clothing makes you forget what a privilege it is to be dressed and that creates complacency.

I have known Masters who find nudity distracting and ask their slaves to wear a thin apron or cover up. That is within the Master's right of course - but ideally the slave would thank the Master for the clothing every day because it is a privilege, not a right.

I also believe a slave is a like a fine bottle of wine in a rack. People keep wine racked so they and others can see it - and know that it's there. Men keep slaves naked to see them and know that at any moment they can drink of the sweet nectar of service found therein.

As a Master, I think so many people in D/s live a double life that I wonder if they miss the fun of socializing with their own kind - beyond the parties- into friendships. What is it like to watch another girl serve? To serve two or more Masters for an afternoon by the pool? What is fun in the slave quarters? Do the Masters trade?

Thank you, Sir for your questions. I do think isolation is detrimental to people who really live as Master/slave or Dom/sub if they are trying to live it with intention. If a couple is a "just in the bedroom" kind of couple - they don't need input or support as much as a couple making a way of life out of their identity - especially if that couple is keeping it a total secret.

Like-minded friends are always good to have. They can share ideas - Masters can support one another, and sister slaves can serve and comfort together. I don't know if Masters trade, but it has been my experience that if a Master is busy, out of town, etc. he can ask a Master friend to administer a whipping or use his woman. Sometimes just hearing a different voice or being spanked in a different pattern can be jarring and good for a slave.

I have had sister slaves serve with me and it's very nice to have the comfort and fellowship around. It may be different for submissives, but for slaves - my experience has been you aren't jealous when your sister slave is serving or allowed to be pleasured because you know it is not her choice. The Master chooses such things and if she is pleasing the Master, you must be happy for the Master. Sister slaves help make the work less, the pleasure more, and it's generally helpful to have another being on my level that I can laugh, share with and get ideas from.

Online blogging makes it seem like slaves spend all day every day locked in the house staring at the Master. That pretty much burns out the couple quickly. Slaves are real people with real lives. There are bills to pay, movies to see, chores to do, dinners to go to, family events to attend, concerts, etc. Having friends who understand both lifestyles and the challenges in between is a huge support, and brings variety into the mix - which is always good. For real life practitioners consensual slavery is more than a bunch of porn slides and fantasy stories online - it's a part of their life, and an experience worth sharing.

My Master wants me to be thin and has been weighing me every week and giving me punishments but I'm not losing any weight. I think I'm rebelling because I am not ready to really submit and he's maybe not the right Master for me. But he just says I'm bratting and trying to get out of the diet cause it's hard. Do you exercise for your Master? Does it help you submit?

———————————〜————————————

Thank you for sharing this concern and question with me. My Master does not tell me what to weigh or to exercise. I exercise for myself. I like being healthy. I work in an office all day long. If I don't exercise I will get weak and not have the strength or muscle tone to do things I love. I enjoy being able to serve him in the Cowgirl position – and that takes a lot of thigh strength and hip flexibility.

My Master cares about me and wants me to be healthy but he accepts me as I am. I'm an adult and he feels like it's not his job to control my health choices. It's my job to make choices and present my body to him. He owns me, but he doesn't micromanage.

Your question does bring out some concerning things. My thoughts would be that the best (and really only way that works) reason for you to lose weight is for you and it has to be your choice.

There are 2 types of motivation – internal (comes from inside of you) and external (comes from someone/something else). For the kind of life change that creates weight loss and strength – it is better to be internal.

If you went to him and said, "I would like to lose weight and I am asking for your help," that would be one thing (and be more likely to work – because the motivation is internal). Then the punishments and diet might be effective. But, having him tell you to lose weight and punishing you if you don't is external and negatively based.

There could be a lot of reasons you are not losing weight. Maybe the diet he picked isn't right for your body type. Maybe the type of exercise you are doing isn't getting your heart rate up enough. Maybe you feel like your Master "wanting you to be thin" is a sign of him not accepting and valuing you as you are – and you resent it.

To me – the larger question is the one at the end – do you want to be his sub? If weight wasn't an issue – is he the person you desire to give yourself to in every way? Once you know whether you desire to offer your submission to him, then you will know what to do.

If you are staying his sub – ask to speak to him and respectfully let him know your true feelings about your weight, diet, and habits. A Dom/sub couple is a team. Work together to achieve what's healthy for you both.

If you aren't sure he's the one – back up and do more training with him, or take a break and make some decisions. If you know he is not the one for you (because of your feelings, not your lack of weight loss), leave gently, peacefully and respectfully.

Does your Master require any rituals or protocols of you?

───────────────── ～ ─────────────────

Thank you for that question. Yes, depending on the situation. Rituals help develop the slave mindset. At his home protocols include:

- Disrobing silently & putting my collar on, placing a paddle on the night table, and kneeling for him to start with a warm up spanking.
- Always silent until spoken to.
- Addressing him properly (Sir, generally; his wife prefers Lady).
- Thanking him after every act of discipline/pain, sex, compliment, or correction.
- If I need to ask him a question starting with, "Please, excuse me, Sir, …" and saying "Thank you, Sir." when he answers.
- The usual "Please" and "Thank you's."
- Kneel beside his chair, hands up and open, unless given a task or permission to use my mouth for his service.
- If I need to engage in self-care, clean myself off, etc., I ask permission to be excused to use the restroom.
- Once he says I am "dismissed," going to the slave quarters (a spare room where he keeps the things associated with my slavery), dressing silently and leaving silently.

Public protocols:

- I dress in a simple long-form black dress and flats. Try to blend into the background as much as possible.
- I open the door for his wife, then him, and then sit in the back of the car (he always drives). Upon

arriving I open the door for his wife then him, then follow closely but always behind them.

- If it is not clumsy or obvious, I will open the door for them. If it is - then he usually holds the door open for us and I thank him upon entry.
- He orders all food, and if the server looks to me I direct the attention to him. (He orders for his wife also).
- At an event I sit on his left side and take my seat only after he sits down. If he stands, I stand (unless he puts his hand on my shoulder indicating I should remain seated.).
- If we are somewhere and they want something they would need to retrieve (glass of wine, napkin at a festival, etc.) I go and bring it to them.
- I eat after they eat or during - once they have started, and I must finish before they do so as to serve them after their meal.

Do you get punished often? If so, how

I am ritually put through pain (belt, whipped, spanked, etc.) although it is not punishment - just pain for his pleasure. I do not require punishment often as I serve my Master at his wishes.

The mindset of the slave is not one that encourages or wants to draw punishment. A "little" will act up or disobey as a form of "bratting" – to get a spanking and attention from her Daddy Dom. A submissive is usually punished as a part of training or testing, or simply correction when she does something wrong. While a slave may be corrected for wrong behavior, we really don't invite or seek punishment. Our internal goal is to please and do everything our Master says the way he says to do it.

That doesn't mean a slave isn't whipped or beaten. We take a tremendous amount of pain under the lash. It simply means I don't get beaten because I did something wrong. I get beaten because I am a slave, and he wants to beat me. Period.

How do you go about preparing for your Friday sessions with your Master? Mentally, physically, etc.

———————————— ～——／————————————

Thank you for asking about my experiences. That's the fun of the community.

Mentally, I use meditation, starting on Thursday night, to calm down and focus. I am always so excited. I imagine going in the door, going into the slave quarters (spare room) waiting for him to come in, etc. That way I can diffuse the frenetic energy and focus on him. I have two mantras I say through the experience. When I'm getting ready - I say in my head over and over, "There is only him…there is only him…there is only him…" focusing my mind on him and nothing else - no matter what is happening at work, at home, or in the world – by the time I get to his house - there is only him.

The second mantra gets me through any fear or pain that I am experiencing and it is simply - "I was born for this." I say it in my head when he enters me or puts an anal hook in me and I'm being stretched or when the nipple clamps finally just start pulsing and aching. I take a deep breath and say, "I was born for this…" and soon I am floating on the pain and the joy of knowing I want this so much…and I'm lucky to have it.

Physically- it's the normal things any woman would do to please a date or mate. I treat every session like someone going on a first date - very precisely and hopefully. So, mani/pedi, hair appointment, tweeze/shave any stray hair or stubble into oblivion, no gastrically challenging food or fruit (asparagus, etc.) starting the day before, etc. Friday morning I take a thorough bath. My family knows Friday is "my personal day" so they aren't surprised when I take extra time to get ready or I'm supernaturally calm.

No matter how much I prepare - I know when I feel the rush of cool air as my clothes come off and I'm naked, waiting for the initial reddening- it's gonna be a flood of emotion each time - and my mouth is usually already watering.

Has your Master ever hurt your feelings, by words or actions, so that you burst into tears in front of him? Do you cry when he spanks you? Does he demand and insist that you cry during your spanking?

———————————————~———————————

    Thank you so much for the awesome questions. In terms of crying - as you might have guessed - I'm not a teary person. I normally only cry real tears when I am very angry, feeling anguish, or watching sappy with puppies or horses. Most things don't bring me to that level.

    My Master doesn't try to hurt my feelings - but maybe twice in three years he said something that did — once he apologized about 2 weeks later (I never mentioned it hurt my feelings, he just said in retrospect it was rude) and once I just forgot about it (so much so I don't remember what he said, just that it took me aback for a moment). No tears either time. I'm more of a rock than a balloon. Very little pops me.

    For spankings, I don't cry. I don't fake it or role play, and I just can't get tears to come out. I gasp, squirm, "worm" my body, breathe heavy, moan, yell, beg, ow...when it is extremely painful I might get to "fight or flight mode" and pull against the restraints. I once bit a penis gag almost in half (we do **not** want to encourage that!). When it passes the fight or flight threshold —- to extreme pain — I have passed out (twice in 20 years) or vomited (several times). Needless to say, My Masters have learned to stop before we get there — and my safe word is usually "I'm going to throw up." Romantic, huh?

    I often see women who kick and wiggle and cry big beautiful tears and I envy them. It looks arousing and fun. I just can't do it.

It wouldn't do any good for him to demand - It's not going to happen. I can't "cry on command" and I think that whole thing is kind of useless. What's the point of crying if I'm making it happen and it's not real? I once had a boyfriend for about a month in grad school who left because I didn't cry and he needed tears to be turned on. It was a bad experience - he beat the hell out of me and not one drop fell from my eyes. I learned to be upfront about the fact - I will definitely suffer for a Master's pleasure and he will see that pain — but - I'm not going to cry. If tears are required - I'm not the slave for him.

As a slave do you love, like or just obey your Master? Do you expect your Master to love or like you?

———————————————⁓—————————————

Thank you for the question. There is an emotion between like and love which I call "bonded." That's what I feel for him. I'm not "in love" with him - like a husband/lover relationship, and I more than "like" him (although I do like and enjoy his company). He enters my body on a regular basis and allows me to take him inside me - that creates a "stronger than like" feeling - which is bonding. I am bonded to him in heart. I deeply care about him and his happiness, health and family, and he does mine.

But - it's not love nor would it be. He's not my "lover" and he doesn't "make love" to me. He uses me. I've seen him make love to his wife, and that's a whole different thing.

Do you crawl for your Master or does that seem too infantile a thing to do at your age?

Thank you for this fun question. Like any slave, I do what my Master says and I don't hesitate to crawl to him if that's what he desires. There is no "infantile" or "other" categories in slavery. There is only obedience.

I spend a lot of time on my knees in his presence and that sometimes means crawling to do something. On occasion he will attach a leash to my collar and make me crawl behind him. I don't mind crawling for him. As long as it is pleasing to him, that's all that really matters.

I'm writing to you because I'm concerned that although my pet adores me as well as serving me, she doesn't worship my cock the way I hoped. She says that she loves its size, etc., but doesn't understand why she would worship it. She just sees it as a part of me, and pleasures it solely to please me. This bothers me because I can't quite reward her just by giving her access to it and because cock worship is a huge turn on. Advice?

———————————

Thank you, Sir for writing me. I am honored you would ask my opinion. I wish you and your pet all good things. My experience has been that no person is everything we want them to be. The best relationships are made of enjoying who we love and all they give us while learning to accept who they are not – even though we might wish it so.

I ask also to say I admire and honor your pet – because she is honest with you. She isn't trying to fake it just to please you – she is telling you the truth. That is worth more than all the pretty lies in the whole world.

Cock worship isn't an action. Cock worship is a philosophy or psychology. It is the idea of valuing the penis for what it is and represents, not just seeing it as a tool for pleasure. I think cock worship comes more naturally from women inclined to follow the ideas of "natural order" – that men have the right to be pleased and honored by women because they are men. To those women – the cock is a symbol of male power and entitlement. As such, the chance to take it in our body is an honor because we are not just pleasing the man – we are embracing his entitlement. A cock isn't just part of your body – it is the emblem of your gender and your power.

For women who don't have that mindset, they can still lavish love and affection on your cock – but the motivation won't be the same. Clearly pleasing you is a desire for her – so reward her by giving her more chances, and more ways to pleasure you. Reward her with praise and affirmation. Reward her for her honesty with your honesty and gentle encouragement. Continue to invest in her mind, her philosophy and motivations, her way of being a pet – and you'll see the "way" and the "why" of her actions grow and develop too.

When you finally get to see your Master, is there a time and place for you to tell him how much you have ached for him? Your suffering is one of his greatest pleasures.

Thank you for this beautiful question. Yes, my Master drinks in my ache like elixir. When I go to serve him next Friday (sooo long it seems) I will disrobe, put on my collar and kneel over the bed waiting for him to come home from work. He will generally start with an OTK warm up before the harsher punishment to redden me begins. He will take his time - rubbing my bare bottom, inserting his fingers into me, caressing my back, playing with my nipples and letting me speak about how very much I desire his cock inside my body and how empty I am without it, how I worship and fixate on his member.

By the time the OTK spanking is complete I am generally babbling like a brook about my desire for him. It prepares both of us for the pain and pleasure to come.

You speak as if the only time you experience joy and pleasure is when you're serving your Master, and not the other way around. Aren't there things he does for you that pleases you? Things that keep you wanting to serve and please him? I admit that I'm not in a BDSM relationship to understand all the dynamics involved, but I can't help but feel that there is more to your relationship and pleasure than him just giving orders and you following them.

Thank you for this thoughtful question. I appreciate your respect and curiosity. A BDSM relationship is like any 3 dimensional object - a picture of it is much different than when you actually hold it in your hand.

First - It **all** pleases me. I get joy of making another person experience pleasure - that's fulfilling. I have a very satisfying sex life where my body is given a lot of attention and fulfillment. I enjoy a medium amount of pain and I have someone willing to spank and give me pain. I enjoy talking with him about sports, telling him about the book I'm reading, sitting with him and his wife at the ballet, symphony, etc. (better than going alone). It's a relationship of respect, fun, sharing, serving and sex - what <u>wouldn't</u> please me about that???

Second — I think you might see too many porn pics and not enough real people. He doesn't "give orders" to me. Not all Masters are misogynists who call women names and treat them like crap. In fact - that's the statistical minority and most of those guys are into fantasy - not reality.

My Master tells me in normal every day tones, "kate, I'd like some coffee." Sometimes when I'm on my game I'll ask him first, "Would you like some coffee, Sir?"

He sits down on the couch and pats his lap. When I lower my head he will guide my mouth to what he wants and I take him inside me. He doesn't actually say, "suck my cock" - it's a gentler, intuitive process. Now, he might grab my hair and gag me with his cock - but that's not unexpected, nor unappreciated.

His sex with me is very rough - because he enjoys that, and I enjoy it as well. I would much rather be taken than made love to - and when it's done I would much rather be dismissed with a playful smack on the rear than cuddled or held.

That might be the part you don't see - when I am naked before him, meeting his needs, enjoying his power over me - I am getting a chance to be exactly who I am without pretense or shame. How many people really do that with their lover/partner/friend?

You wear a dog collar? With a leash hook? I always thought you would wear something more elegant. Does your Master ever really put a leash on you? Isn't that more a "pet" than a "slave?"

———————— ~~~ ————————

Thank you for your questions. I am very humbled that you think I might wear a more elegant collar, but I am not an elegant lady. I'm a consensual slave - owned by a Man for the purpose of his sexual gratification and domestic service. Aesthetically, I like simple things, common things, and I find beauty in them.

The leash hook serves many purposes. My Master does hook a leash to it. (It matches the collar, and is always in his possession, never mine). He also will sometimes run the chain of my nipple clamps through it, or even the chain to an anal hook. When he is in a fun mood he has hooked my leash to it, run the leash between my breasts, between my vaginal lips (So that it pushes up against my clit), then through my legs - connecting to the spreader bar from the back. So every movement gives my leash and clitoris a good tug.

My Master enjoys having me walk behind him on my hands and knees as he holds my leash, and likes taking me from behind while pulling the leash tight. We attend conventions together on occasion and I am always leashed (although walking upright) at those events. On rare summer days when my parents are visiting my aunts and the girls are not home, he enjoys walking me on the leash around my property (I own several acres of woods around my house and guest house), gathering switches (shudder). The collar is an "always" presence, the leash more of a special occasion - although we both wish it was used more.

I view the collar and leash as a yin/yang. The collar is my bond, the symbol of my identity as a slave. It is always on my neck, and shows my consensual captivity to his will. The leash is his power, the symbol of his guidance, leadership and entitlement. The leash is always in his hand, it stays in his pocket and his house. It shows his bondage of me in will, body and destiny. I would feel incomplete if we used one and not the other.

We don't get caught up in labels and rules - what is a pet, or sub, or lg, or slave. I do what he tells me and he does what he likes with me.

I'm a sub and I've been struggling recently with communicating my needs. I fail to see the line between healthy communication and imposing a rhythm and a frame to our relationship. I want to follow his orders and I'm fairly new at this and wonder: he knows my limits, but am I supposed to express my desires and needs? Is it a question of form or am I topping from the bottom?

Thank you so much for your question. I think one of most confused and misunderstood phrases in all of BDSM is "topping from the bottom." - Untrained/new Dominant people often use it when their sub is challenging them or asking something of them — but that is not what that means. It's not a magic button designed to make a sub "shut up and do what the Dom says."

"Topping from the bottom" means the person assuming the submissive role (whether for a night or for a relationship) is actually the one in charge - giving orders or purposefully manipulating the situation to give her the power.

"Topping from the bottom" does not mean:
- Setting a limit
- Saying when something hurts
- Expressing concern or fear about a command
- Expressing desires, feelings, wants or needs
- Speaking out against unfairness, violation of agreements or abuse
- Bringing ideas to the table
- Doing something with uniqueness or initiative

"Topping from the bottom" is about taking or asserting power. Communication is about sharing, connecting and collaborating.

For example: If I said to my Master - "Look, I've served a month without an orgasm so today I better get one." That would be "topping from the bottom" (and a good way to ensure I served another month without one).

If I said, "Sir, I have served a month without an orgasm and I am very sexually tense. I ask you to consider allowing me to have one this weekend." Then, I am expressing my need and concern.

If I said, "That cane on the thigh thing hurt like crap. You're not hitting me with that again!" It would be power-taking.

If I said, "Sir, the cane on the inner thigh created a pain that took me days to heal from and I found it very painful." I have communicated the truth so he can hear it. I'm not taking any power.

Attitude intentions are what make something "topping from the bottom." Masters who value their subs and slaves actively listen to their needs, desires and feelings. That way the Master knows the heart of the sub and can act accordingly. Masters who do not allow listening sessions or ways for a slave/sub to speak freely without fear (but with respect) - are not creating relationship - they are just acting out a selfish scene.

Do you and your Master think the same about everything? Like football games or politics? During the Super Bowl this friend asked me which team I liked and I said I grew up in Florida so I like the Dolphins. My Dom told him I was dumb and that WE liked the Cowboys. He said if he likes the Cowboys then I have to like them too and gave me swats and made me say the Cowboys were the best team after every swat. I didn't mind it but it seems weird my mind is just supposed to change.

Thank you for your thoughts and sharing this question with me. I have to tell you it gives me some concerns I would like you to hear. But first, your answer.

No, my Master and I do not think the same about everything. He doesn't try to change me and I don't try to change him. We have playful bets (winning team gives losing a back rub) but that's about it. We accept each other as we are.

I think the idea "feels weird" to you because it is wrong. People don't just change their personality, identity and preferences because someone says so. Part of owning a slave (or Domming a sub) is understanding you have power over a <u>person</u> – not a robot, blank slate, or piece of clay. You do not change your slave into a copy of yourself – that's narcissism (a type of unhealthy self-obsession and self-seeking). You own the slave as she is and you enjoy what she offers you.

Truthfully, Sister Servant, your question gives me a lot of concern. I feel it is a red flag about the health of your relationship. My knee-jerk reaction is to say "that's abusive" but – I try to not to judge people or situations I don't know and didn't see.

What I will tell you is my feeling that this story - as I read it - falls on a line. At one end is "Untrained/Misunderstands" and at the other end is "abusive". It is possible your Dom is making this up as he goes along and has never been trained on what Dominance and submission is or what is appropriate to do or not do. He may be misunderstanding his position and think it gives him the right to change your likes and dislikes. On the other end is abusive. Find his behavior on the line, and if it is abusive, make plans or get help to leave.

What if a slave had a Master that is a wonderful dominant, but through a series of unfortunate events outside his control, he became depressed, unmotivated, and basically feels less of a man. Do you think it's possible for a slave to restore her Master back to a position of dominance? To make him feel like the man he is meant to be?

———————————⟋◠◠⟍———————————

Thank you for your question. That is a serious and emotionally trying situation. Consensual slavery is made of adults, and in the adult world - real life, with its joy and issues, is always going to take priority. The reality is that the Master, as an adult, is the one responsible for his emotions and his healing. A slave can't do it, and shouldn't bear the responsibility.

Every adult is responsible for their own feelings and mental health. If a Master is depressed, then the Master needs to take steps toward health, including a medical exam and/or psychotherapy. If the Master won't seek help, then the slave must consider changing the scope of the relationship to a less dependent/vulnerable position. You can still love and be with someone who is not mentally healthy, but you should not rely on that person for the kind of decision making done in Master/slave relationships. If he is struggling to uphold and control himself, he can't control you.

But, no. The slave cannot "make him feel like a man" or a Master. That has to come from within him. If he is in a bad season, then he must make the effort necessary (perhaps including taking time off from power exchange) to heal it.

I don't like sucking guys or the taste of cum. Does that mean I can't be a slave?

———————~———————

Thank you for this question. It is not for me to say who is or is not a slave. The internet is full of people who will judge you or define you for whatever you do or don't, but no one can tell you who you are. That is for you to know. I am a slave. That is all I know without question. But, here are my thoughts on your question.

I think you might be approaching the question backwards. You are looking at the external (sucking men) to confirm the internal (slavery). But it is really the other way around. Slavery is internal (your attitude, not your action) that shows through the external (kneeling, sucking, respect).

I didn't say, "I love giving oral service and anal sex so I'm a slave." What I said was, "I know I need to be owned. I don't wish to be independent or empowered. I was born to serve men. I am a slave." So - oral service and anal sex are ways men may use me.

Look at your heart. There are a lot of things to be: There is consensual slavery (an enslaved, lower being), there is submission (a free woman who gives control of herself to men), there is little girl, Slut, "princess by day/whore by night", spanking/discipline subject - all kinds of definitions. Find who you are then be honest and communicate to your potential Master just exactly what you want to be and do.

If you are a slave - then you have no choice in oral service. It doesn't really matter if you like it or not, you'll do it. It is possible you might be taken on as a sister slave to a Master who has a willing cock servant. Then you can serve in other ways. But if the Master wants your mouth, he will have it.

If you are a submissive - you can set limits and rights with your submission. It's possible you might find a Master who accepts "no oral" as a limit (although, I'm willing to bet his first goal will be to stretch that limit). If you are another identity - you have more negotiating power.

So pick the road you want to walk (or take time to learn more) then see where it may lead you. I must say - oral service is one of the basics in sexual service. What you're saying is like saying, "I want to be an artist's assistant but I don't like the smell of paint and I don't want to clean brushes." You are choosing a hard path to deny a Master your mouth. But a hard path doesn't mean it is an impossible path.

There is a place for everyone in service. Find your place and the rest will get settled.

My husband came out as a Dom several years ago but sadly, I'm not as submissive as he'd like. Your arrangement with your Master and his wife is my perfect fantasy! Where does one find a slave such as yourself? Obviously, kate, you need to be cloned!

―――――――――〜〜〜〜―――――――――

     I saw this very late at night - but it made me laugh out loud at the idea of being cloned. Thanks for that. Laughter is a great gift to give. I do believe if you asked my sisters, my cousins, my employees and my mailman they would all tell you one kate is all the world can take. But I do appreciate the thought.

     How courageous of you to encourage your husband as a Dom, and work to find solutions for the parts that aren't as smooth as they can be. That is beautiful. I have all respect and honor for my Master's wife – she allows another woman into her home, to be used by her husband to meet his needs. What a great strength and love she must have for him.

     I am on the underside of this coin, but I believe the first step in finding a sub or slave to enhance your husband's dominance is found between you two. Sit down and honestly discuss what that scenario would look and feel like. Do you want to be involved at all? Is she going to serve you both or just him? What are the limits you both feel good about in terms of him having a sub/slave who is not you? Before you go looking – get a really good idea of what you want to catch.

     Then, the best place to look is your local BDSM community – or people within your locality range. Your Dom/husband should tell the sub/slave the truth up front – it's not going to be love – but it is service, training, and experiences. There are many women who may be willing to

serve a married man or couple - you just need to meet them
– and be fair and honest with them.

I just recently discovered I am a Master and enjoy spanking/dominating women. I have been showing her BDSM blogs. She doesn't like it. I told her if she can't be the woman I need, then I will have to get another to spank and fuck. She says that would be having an affair and she would divorce me. Do you think it is an affair? How can I make her like it?

Thank you for this question, Sir. This is a very serious issue and I am going to list several short thoughts and encourage you to work this out offline with your wife. It doesn't matter if I think it is an affair or not. What matters is what it is between you two. As you asked my opinion, here is my thinking.

1. You can't make her like it. Either she is into this life or she isn't. Submission, consensual slavery, spanking, - it is all based on the interest and consent of the women involved. If she isn't interested, the rest of it shouldn't happen.

2. Many women are interested in some level of kink, but need to discover that organically. It's possible she is really overwhelmed. Showing her blogs featuring chained women with cum on their breasts, painful face-fucking, and humiliation isn't a great starting place. It's like starting a student driver by dropping her on a NASCAR track. Get offline and talk about adding a little spanking to your sex life. If she is willing, begin slow and give her a taste of the fun side of kink.

3. I think you have an incomplete idea, as well. Spanking and fucking a woman doesn't make you a Master. That's a whole psychology of itself. It is possible you are suddenly attracted to this life because you are feeling a

need for control of other areas. Take time to develop an ideology of what it means to be a Master before ruining your marriage over it.

Porn isn't real. A lot that you see online isn't real (in fact, a lot of these young women saying "I want daddy's cock in my ass" are actually still virgins or have only had an "online" daddy, not a physical experience). People you meet on dating sites aren't usually real. Your marriage is real. See a counselor together or spend time exploring sexual options before demanding something she can't give, and losing what you already have.

You seem so nice so I thought you might help and not judge. I've been submitting online to a Dom and he is coming here next week in person. Online I wrote all these things I wanted him to do to me like beat me with a belt and take my ass. But I've never been spanked in any way and I've only had regular sex a few times, never anal. I'm terrified because I wrote all these "when you get here emails" that are so much more than I can really do. Now he's coming. I don't want to cancel but I'm so scared. What do I do?

Thank you for writing me and sharing your situation. I am sure you feel a lot of pressure and concern right now. The first thing to do is relax. Take some deep breaths and remember a few things:

- All submission in BDSM is consensual. You have a right to say, "No."
- You still have control of your body and mind until you choose to give it away.
- You have the power to stop anything you can't endure.
- You have the ability to change the game plan if you need.
- You have the obligation to be honest.

I believe if you are going to bare your body and give it to this man, you first should be honest with him about the situation. To me, the experience is meaningless if it is done without truth.

Since online communication is your norm - I think it is also a way to start your togetherness out fresh. Tell him that you are deeply entranced by his power and you've let your mind and lustful thoughts get away from you. Let him know the truth - you want to meet him and you want to do all those things you wrote — but they have to happen in time. Let him know you are new and he will need to begin more slowly. Tell him that the things you wrote were a vision and a goal and something to work toward - but they are near the finish line and you are at the starting gate.

If he is an experienced Dom, he is going to start you off slowly anyway - because almost all Doms start with an OTK spanking that builds so they can measure your pain tolerance and start with oral or vaginal sex to get used to your body and to train it to please him.

If he has only been an online Dom - then this is a good chance for him to learn the difference between online desire and real life reality. Neither one is better than the other - but they are different. Learning to start out slowly is a good habit for him to get into.

I hope all goes well for you both and remember - there is a time for all the things you wrote about - if you want them - you two are just going to have to work your way there - like all the rest of us.

Is it ever appropriate to lie to your Master? Even for a noble reason such as to spare his feelings?

———————————— ⌇ ————————————

Thank you for asking this. It is sensitive and a good question. There isn't a lot written or spoken about slave ethics beyond service and obedience. But, I think the understood thought is that a slave is honest with their owner out of principle. I find the more honest we are with the world around us, the better life is, even when the truth makes it momentarily harder.

It is also a question of trust. If you trust your Master with your body and fate, allowing him to own you, you should also be able to trust him to master his own feelings and own them. No one is responsible for what another person does with their feelings.

Finally - most people lie out of fear. That is never a good reason to do anything in a relationship. Serve your Master out of love, obedience, pleasure, exploration, respect - but never out of fear.

I think, whenever it is at all possible, it is better to tell the truth lovingly, rather than out-and-out lie. For example, if a Master says, "Do you like it when we have anal sex after a spanking?" If the truth is you don't - you can say, "It isn't my favorite thing but I like the pleasure it gives you." Suppose he has the kind of personality that drives others away - and asks you, "Do you think there's something wrong with me?" Instead of saying, "Yes, you're abrasive and rude sometimes." You can say, "I think people expect a different type of communication than you give, and it causes a rift."

A slave's words should be as soft as her body.

There's a lot of pressure to be or become everything the Master wants you to be - but I feel it is wiser to be everything you are (even if it sometimes conflicts with the

Master's feelings) and serve him with everything you are.
If it is not enough/not right - then your pairing is not a good
one, and he may not be your destiny.

Hello lovely kate. Does a slave have a right to ask for exclusivity from her Master or any man for that matter?

———————————— ~~~~~ ————————————

Thank you for the beautiful note. This is a hard question. I think conversations about exclusivity, sharing, disease protection, limits and life expectations are all very important. Ideally, though - they should happen before the slave is indentured to the Master/Owner. That way - it is not a slave asking/telling the Master how to live — but a woman telling a man what environment her slavery thrives best in.

First - the slave must know herself. Some women don't mind if a Master has other women, or shares her with other men (safety protocols in place). Other women are raised in monogamy and really need to be with a man who will only be with her. No matter which type of woman the slave is - share that with a Master upfront.

Consent should be based on the best match. Remember - this kind of slavery is <u>consensual.</u> The slave has the right to choose who Masters her. So, if a Master says he has no desire for only one slave and she realizes monogamy is her need - she shouldn't consent to him.

Slaves don't have to be owned by every man in the room, but they must treat every free man and free woman with respect. Once a slave consents to a Master as his slave - all future consent is considered offered - so make sure to get as much clarity up front as possible.

I consider myself a submissive woman and when my partner says I am his property this is correct. He will not allow me to have any other male sexual partners than him but he can do as he wishes (of course). I admire your servant's heart and wish that I did not feel a tinge of sadness that he wishes to be sexual with others. Is there any advice or help that you can give? I want to give him whatever he wishes with sincerity. We are deeply in love and I want only his happiness.

Dear Sister Servant,

I am honored that you would ask me this question, and feel for your sadness. I try not to give advice to others, as every person is different - but I can give you my perspective (and what my choice might be & what my experience has been) on the situation you shared with me, which I want to assure you is something many submissives and slaves feel. You are not alone in the situation or the sadness.

My perspective is that your Master owns all of you. That includes your body (sexually and personally), your will (decisions you make), your circumstances (discipline or reward) and your emotions. Your sadness is his responsibility also - as you are his property. As such, it is in your Master's best interest that you share your feelings with him in an appropriate way, just as you give your body to him.

In a situation like this I would ask for permission to speak to him honestly (most wise Masters have a protocol or form of communication time to listen to their slaves or subs) and tell him I affirm his right to determine his sexuality and mine, but I feel a sadness when he has sex with others. Then I would listen to him.

If you were raised in western culture, chances are you were raised to think of monogamy as the norm. It takes time to shed that idea - if you want to shed it at all. My best thought is nothing bad comes from speaking truth and love to a Master. Even if he reacts angrily, it gives you a chance to explore the idea and gives him a chance to be a true Master - not just a spanker/sex partner.

In the two main long-term Master/slave relationships I have had I was the only house slave, but my Masters did have sex with other women at play parties, training new subs/slaves or providing a service to another Master by using his sub/slave, etc. I understood it was just sex - as a tool or as a pleasure and not a withdrawal from me. At the end of the night, I was beside the Master's bed or invited to the bed with him. I was also told up front in both cases that it would happen.

It is impossible for me to say for sure, because I have never been, and never want to be a Master. But, when I read your comments - I believe if I were a Master, I would want to know those things - that you loved me, that you wanted my happiness, but that you felt sadness and we needed to address that emotion. Being a slave doesn't mean you can't communicate and share thoughts and ideas.

Dear kate, I have been a slave at heart for as long
as I remember. Ever since I was a little girl I knew
I wanted a Master. I have someone I love dearly
set in mind but he lives a couple time zones away.
He thinks I'd be fitting as an odalisque. My two
questions are: is it okay as a slave, to set in a
contract that Master can't be with another girl?
And can it work even if not in person at the
moment?

Hello Sister Slave,
   You clearly have had a slave heart for a long time.
The Code D' Odalisque is a very ritualized form of sexual
slavery - very, very different from the things you see
online. It has to do with a beauty aesthetic, pleasure only,
and seclusion. (It is based on the Eastern Harem ideals -
beautiful women kept as pleasure slaves).
   As far at the contract about other women - it would
be unusual, and your Master would set the contract, not
you. The only bargaining power a slave has in consensual
slavery is consent. So, if you cannot serve a man who is
with other women - you must tell him that you cannot
consent to be his slave without that promise and ask it to be
part of your contract or understanding. If he agrees - then it
is good. If he disagrees - then you have to make a decision
about whether or not to consent to be his slave.
   Long distance things can work; do work - but they
also take work. An Odalisque is kept in seclusion and used
only for sexual pleasure - since there is no discipline (one
never whips an odalisque) or training other than how to
please your Master - it can work if you two Skype or do
whatever you need to make sure you are always pleasing to
him, look appropriate: naked, barefoot, hair, eyes, makeup

perfect — think "Geisha" only one who has sex (traditional Geisha's don't have sex; they are aesthetic only).   So with time, communication, etc., it can work for a while.

Is financial slavery part of your current slavery?
How does that work for you and has it worked
differently for you with past Masters?

―――――――――――

Thank you for this question. When I was married to my husband/Master financial slavery was indeed part of the marriage. I would bring home my check, kneel before him and give it to him. He made the major monetary decisions, paid bills out of the account, etc. That was very important to our power exchange because I made a significant amount more than he did so it helped to put the money in the account and have him manage it.

That can work the other way as well. Two years before the end of our marriage he was engaged in prescription drug addiction that left him unable to make good decisions regarding money/assets, etc. We decided to change the accounts so we ran the house, benefits, and important things out of my account and he had his own account. I kept up with the bills and gave him an accounting of the payment every month - as a responsible house steward would do. So - if the Master in the relationship is not a great money manager - the slave can ensure the household needs and show the accounting to her Master.

After my divorce I bought a good sized property, and became fully financially responsible for myself, my elderly parents who live in my guest house, and then my sister (help with education) and my sister's children who live with me by court order. My second Master had no interest in dealing with those finances since I didn't live with him and I was self-reliant.

My current Master has a wife and home and is happy for me to run my own household, as my service to him is bi-weekly, and occasional special sessions and not

24/7 - (although I am his slave 24/7 in spirit and mind).
So, again, no financial slavery is required.

The key to consensual slavery – not just financially – is to really look at the situation you exist in. Do you live together or is this session work? Who has the better ability to pay bills and run finances? How can it be designed to complement your slavery? Communication and planning make financial slavery possible.

When you prepare a festive dinner for your Master and his wife, do you pay for it (even when they give you the recipes and suggest the menu)? I realize you are a slave of "independent means" serving a well-to-do couple, but not all slaves are in that situation. You gave great advice to a slave on a budget who wanted to make a special meal for her Master. But your situation seems different, at least economically.

Thank you for your question and compliment. Usually the only things I pay for are things I want that are fresh or special. Most of the time if they have told me what they want – I will tell or email my Master or the Lady and tell them what foods are necessary to prepare it. The ingredients will be in the kitchen when I arrive. So – they pay for most of the meal.

What I end up paying for is if I want something extra (like a decoration, or a fine wine I'd like them to try), fresh cutlets from the butcher, or dessert. I see my payment of those things as being responsible for my end of the decisions. If I want to garnish her plate with edible orchids, then I should pay for them – it's a gift. If they are just going to have wine, I can use any bottle they have that pairs well. If I want them to try a certain wine, then I buy it – again, a gift. I pay for dessert because I don't know how to make pastries well – so I am providing it. Sometimes I pick up flowers for the table. All of that, in essence, are gifts of devotion from me to them – so I pay for them.

You are correct that not all slaves have the finances to put out money for such things. If that is the case, then a wise Master won't put the slave in a position where spending money is expected or will reimburse for what is needed. If a slave can't afford to give food, then the Master should ask what the costs of the meal are up front, and give the slave that money to do her work. As I said before – you don't have to spend a lot of money in order to provide your Master a luxurious meal. Personal responsibility, understanding and generosity make a slave's life good.

You mentioned that if your Master buys your ticket for you to go with them to a concert, you present him a check for the cost while on your knees. I'm sure it's a beautiful gesture. What does it mean? When you presented your Master/husband with your paycheck on your knees you were acknowledging that you worked outside the home with his permission. But now you work for your family, not your current Master. Could you explain the difference between these two (beautiful) gestures of submission?

Thank you for this question. Meaning has so much importance in choices we make as Masters and slaves. When I was married, I gave my husband my paycheck because, as head of household, he handled our money and I offered my labor and the fruit of my labor to him. Later in the marriage when he was no longer able to be the financial leader of our relationship, I took it over and gave him a report each month to be accountable (he didn't read it, but I gave it to him). So – those gestures honor my slavery and my role as wife. In marriage – it was all his (our) money – no matter who made it.

However, I am not married to my current Master and so my money is my money and his money is his money. Although we are friendly, I am also not his "friend" – I am his slave. When he tells me he wants me at a symphony performance – he isn't inviting a friend – there's no reason he should buy my ticket. Serving him is a privilege (and fun) and I am willing and able to pay to do it. I give him the check on my knees – paying for my own ticket, which is proper, - but also showing by my attitude that I am grateful to have a chance to serve him in that way. When I buy his and his wife's tickets because of my membership discounts he leaves the money for me – but doesn't present it to me ceremonially or really even mention it – because he's the Master.

Money can make or break a relationship whether it's a marriage, friendship or service relationship. It is always important to know what money means, and what it doesn't mean. Keeping the concept of money in its proper place is essential for a healthy BDSM relationship.

Pleasure and Pain

The Slave Speaks

You never appreciate the sweet until you've had the sour. The life of a consensual slave is filled with both. BDSM is a connective relationship built on trust, love, discipline and delight. It's not all just sex and spankings – but – there's a lot of expression that comes from those two elements. Being used sexually is a part of the package. Let's face it. If all my Master wanted me to do was fold his laundry and wash some windows – he'd get a maid. Sexuality is a service the consensual slave will offer and expect. Pain is also something the slave will experience on a regular basis. His power over you don't just include the power to boss you around. He has the power and the obligation to discipline and guide you –as well as engage in some good ole' fashioned kinky whips and canes. Slave life – at the very best of its moments - is found in the balance between pleasure and pain.

Every person has things they like to do sexually and things they really can't stand. When you consent to a man to be his slave – you'll do both. Sexuality in M/s usually begins with oral service and works itself all the way to anal intercourse. For Masters who enjoy more control over their slave the scale is spread even farther apart. On one side there is enforced chastity, where a slave is not allowed to touch herself or orgasm without her Master's permission, and on the other is forced orgasm, where a slave is bound and repeatedly stimulated until her body reacts. The point of all that tension and exhaustion is ownership. A Master doesn't simply own your actions, he owns your sex as well.

Every coupling is different. Is it possible to be a sub or slave and not have anal sex? Of course it is. What if you are willing to give oral sex but it makes you gag and you don't like it? What about other forms of pleasure – enemas, breast biting or just some dirty talk before bed? All of those are questions people ask. By far, however, the most anguished questions I receive are from women who do not want their Master to be sexual with others, and wonder what they can do about it. The answer to all those questions is very often the same one: communication.

Apart from the sweet pleasure of sex is the sting of pain. Pain comes to a consensual slave in many forms – the discipline of training, the spankings and rituals of eroticism and the blistering endurance of the cane, the single tail and the wooden pony. Suffering for your Master is as much a part of serving him as cuddling up after sex or washing his dishes. Not all Masters thrive on testing their slaves with pain, but many find it a fulfilling and sexy part of submission. Most women who choose to be consensual slaves enjoy a medium or high amount of pain and love the challenge to endure it.

When I kneel before my Master I never know if I am going to be opening my body to his pleasure or enduring lashes from his belt. All I know is when it's over I will kneel before him once more and say, "Thank you."

I know you practice chastity when you aren't with your Master. You always talk like chastity is a good thing. I hate it. It makes me angry, moody, and I end up begging then demanding relief. Then I get punished for forgetting my place. What good could chastity possibly do for you?

Thank you for this note and sharing your feelings with me. It can definitely be hard to deal with, but just because something is hard doesn't mean it isn't doing good things for you. Things chastity does for me:

It makes me know I'm owned. I'm an educated, empowered woman with a good job, property, entitlements - and I can't even touch my own body. Chastity is that part that says, "You are not your own." That's powerful stuff.

Chastity shows my obedience and loyalty. I see all these "tests" Masters put slaves through - wear this, do that, write an email every day, kneel on this rice for an hour reciting my name, etc. - and we don't have to spend time on that. He knows I am obedient, even when my clit has become a throbbing ball of lava between my legs - because I will not relieve my discomfort without approval.

Chastity gives me more energy and attention. I have had several special events to serve my Master and the Lady this month so I've seen him more than normal - but I've been kept chaste through those events. Thus - every time he touches me, my body reacts.

Chastity gives me practice in mental discipline. I have a lot of responsibility. I can't walk around thinking about orgasm all day. So I have to learn to get my mind off my need and focus. It's a great practice ground for mental discipline.

And finally - when I am allowed to climax — it's fantastic. (As a bonus in both the suffering and sexy part - chastity also gives me amazing sex dreams).

Every woman is different and responds to control in a different way. My way has been acceptance and gratitude, and it works for me.

May I ask, in what form have you been kept in chastity? A belt? For how long? How does the belt affect you?

———————————～———————————

Thank you for asking. Chastity belts are actually one of my favorite things - although they are not practical for me to wear much of the time.

I am kept under the requirement of chastity anytime I am not serving my Master. I can think all the luscious thoughts I want, but no touching.

That is usually done by honesty and personal discipline. I do have a stainless steel chastity belt with inline lock that I was measured for and fits wonderfully. However, even though the lock is inline it shows through my work clothes and would not be wise for me to wear daily. I generally wear it if I accompany my Master to an event or he and his wife to a festival for when we are out and about - as just a reminder that I am an owned person. So - my belt is more fun than actually preventative.

When I feel him pull it tight and lock it and then watch as he puts the key in his pocket – it is the biggest thrill — whether I'm wearing it through a movie - or for a day.

When you write that your Master has the key to your chastity belt, does it mean you wear it all the time when not in his presence? Would it not be a little dangerous (medical emergencies, etc.)?

———————— ∽ ————————

Thank you for this question and allowing me to be clear. I only wear my chastity belt ceremonially (at the poker game, or when he tells me to wear it around the house during my service, when we are out of town, or sometimes when we are at a festival or place my dress and blouse hide the fact it is on me. I place it on, lock it into place, kneel before him and hand him the key (that is such a rush it never gets old — handing another person the key to your sex). I love it - if I could, I would wear it most of the time — I just don't have a life that accommodates that.

I keep chastity all other times by not touching myself and honoring that my body is my Master's property. The belt is just an outward symbol of the inward truth.

In medical emergencies there really isn't a problem. EMS personnel or ER docs don't go looking for the key (even though a lot of 24/7 people have a key holder number on theirs). If they needed to remove it - they would just cut the lock or cut it off of you. They don't care how many hundreds of dollars you spent on it. If your life depends on them getting to your pelvic area (not a lot of emergencies require them to access you vaginally) or taking off the belt so you can have an MRI — they cut it off. EMS First Responders see all kinds of interesting things - they wouldn't blink twice.

Would you ever text your Master and ask him to
let you orgasm? What if you needed release really
bad?

─────────────────〜─────────────────

Thank you for this interesting question. I would
never text my Master about that. I accept my bonds of
chastity and value what chastity brings to my life - even
when it is difficult. Chastity does good things for an owned
woman - to the heart and the head as well as the body - and
I honor his right to restrict me far more than I would value
release.

Besides, if I ask - it takes away his ability to give
me that gift on his own - which would be a sweeter and
better moment.

I want to be able to suck my Dom a lot longer like cock worship but my jaw hurts and I have to quit after a few minutes. It frustrates him because he ends up finishing himself off. How can you make it last without your jaw falling off?

————————————⌇————————————

Thanks for asking me this question about what is clearly one of my favorite topics — fellatio! I love cock worship and with the right circumstances can spend an entire afternoon sucking and worshiping my Master's beautiful cock. What are the right circumstances?

1. Movement - jaws aren't made to be in one position - they are hinges - meant to move. When you lock your jaw to hold your mouth open for his cock you are setting yourself up for pain. Move around. Lick the shaft - starting at the base, running up the back with your tongue then encapsulating the head in your mouth. Kiss and lick him, sucking the head (that's where the nerve endings are), then opening up to take his shaft in your mouth and throat. Don't just move your head back and forth. Purse your lips, flick your tongue and let your jaw move.

2. Back support - part of the reason your jaw hurts is you are stiffening your neck to support your back in an "on your knees" position. If you are going to worship his cock for a long time, try lying on a couch with your head in his lap, or sucking him while he is seated and you rest your body on his legs or brace on the arms of a chair — anything that can support your back so your jaw and shoulders can be loose and comfortable. My favorite thing is when he is watching a show and he allows me to just keep my head in his lap, licking, kissing and honoring his member.

3. More than Mouth – if he doesn't prefer you to use your hands to hold or rub his penis (some men think it's

cheating – but that's silly – when they deny your hands they are denying themselves more sensations) then use your hands to fondle his balls between kissing and sucking them, wrap them around him and massage his buttocks, or rub his thighs. If you can take enough of him in your mouth to put your head on his abdomen, rub your nose against him or your cheeks on his legs – use every part of your body you can. Cock worship isn't just sucking – it's worship – it's giving your whole self to his power, using every resource, praising him and luxuriating him.

Finally – if you do have to stop – I hope you will encourage your Dom to allow you to finish him to climax in another way – with your hands or between your breasts, or in some way that pleasures him for that final rally.

Any tips for swallowing my Master's cum, even though it disgusts me?

Thanks for asking me this question. I am sorry the taste disgusts you, as I am sure it makes this process harder. There are a lot of factors that you can employ to help with this so I'll list a few and if you've tried them, please forgive the redundancy. I wish I had a magic button to make his seed a better experience for you. I don't mind the taste and I just tell myself, "This is part of him and I want him inside me."

1. Always be honest. If you are new to swallowing or are still learning to swallow tell your Master that fact. A caring Master can take steps to help you learn to swallow or at least be patient as you grow and experiment in this area. Make sure your Master always knows you are not rejecting him in any way. (Many men feel if you won't swallow or you don't like their cum you are rejecting them and it hurts their feelings. Actually, if someone gave me oral sex then spit in a tissue, I'd be a little insulted too).

2. You haven't said what disgusts you - if it is the texture (how it looks or feels) in total - ask him to ejaculate on your breasts or in your hands to play with it and get used to it. If it is the taste - then there are a number of other remedies (see below).

3. There is an internet myth that if he drinks pineapple juice it will taste sweet. While there may be a small increase, the truth is he would have to drink gallons of it to make a noticeable effect, so don't bother changing his diet (high sulfur foods like asparagus do make it more acidic and sour, however, so be aware).

4. If taste is the issue and you are able to accommodate his penis in the back of your mouth, have him push back to your throat when he is about to ejaculate - that way it goes right down your throat and you won't taste

it as much because it's past the taste buds. The first time you try that you're going to gag or feel it - but eventually you get used to the sensation. You'll get less taste this way than if you spit it out, anyway.

5. Keep it in perspective. Although the porn pictures and blogs make it seem like gallons of the stuff is coming out - the reality is the average male ejaculation is 10CC (or one spoonful). Don't let your perception tell you it's going to be a ton - because it the same as taking a spoonful of chlorine tasting cough syrup - down and done! The rest of the liquid in the process is actually your saliva - and you swallow that hundreds of times a day.

6. Eat a handful of mints, Altoids, or cinnamon disk prior to your service - that will give your mouth a lasting flavor that will lessen (and sometimes overcome) the taste of his ejaculate. If you use one of the chilling type of mints, it will also provide a fun sensation during fellatio. Or, keep some mints on hand for after. Trust me - popping a few tic tacs in your mouth is much nicer to your Master than brushing your teeth afterward.

7. There are a number of chemical sprays and agents to help women with their gag reflex or taste issues. I tend to avoid those because they become a crutch in the process that is hard to give up. However, if you feel it will help you get started - you can give them a try.

My Dom is angry with me because I don't like the way his cum tastes. I do what he says, but he knows I don't like it. How do you hide the fact you hate his cum?

————————⌇————————

Thank you for this question, Sister Servant. Personally, I enjoy giving oral pleasure and part of that pleasure is swallowing the natural outcome. So, I don't mind the way cum tastes, but I don't really dwell on it either.

I see cum as a gift. It is the Master's reward for pleasuring him. If someone gave you a gift, you wouldn't hold it up and say, "I don't really like this." In fact, when I hold a dinner party and a guest brings a bottle of wine I don't like I don't hold it up and say, " I don't like the way this tastes." I thank them for the wine. Sometimes I serve it to guests with the offer of other wines. That way I can drink the wine I want and so can they. Sometimes I am just polite and drink it. It is bad form to be rude about a gift.

I think the same is true with this: You are the servant and you have a couple of choices:

1. Endure. You may not like the taste of cum, but take it, swallow it and be done. Talking about how it tasted is very rude. It makes the Master feel unwanted.

2. Offer alternatives. Encourage your master to mark you on your face, breasts, etc. with his cum. Note: cum in eyes can sting (I find that much more difficult to endure than the taste).

3. Speak to your Master honestly and tell him that you are having trouble with the taste. He may decide you just need to get used to it and give you a lot of chances to swallow it - or he may find ways to work around the concern and pull out before ejaculating in your mouth.

No matter what you decide - do it with respect, and make sure he doesn't feel unwanted or insulted.

Have you ever sucked a dick in public or do you use the "I'm too high profile" excuse to get out of it?

―――――――――――――――――――〜――――――――――――

      Thank you for your blunt question. I have given oral service in public - Usually in cities I do not live, and always in places where children are not going to come across such a display. Perhaps the most public would be at all adult beaches or adult-only resorts. But also, places like rest-stops (with Master acting as a look out for police and children), the back row of movie theaters, camping, hotel suites, lots of parked cars/backseats and fetish bars/parties.

      The second part of the question hurts my heart. I can't imagine "getting out of it" using any reason. First, I am a consensual slave and it is not appropriate for a slave to "get out of" anything. Second, I adore and worship the Master's cock and am more likely to beg to nurture it in my mouth than to ever deny it. That would be like denying ambrosia.

      It is true that most slaves have to think about their public reputation and make arrangements accordingly. That's just real life and nothing a wise Master would prohibit.

Dear kate: Your description of serving with a sister slave was intense. You get to feel her pleasure as well as his. In such moments does your passion ever become general - as in 'I love men', or 'I love cock' - in addition to what you feel for your Master?

———————————————〜〜—————————————

Thank you for this question. I love to have the Master's cock inside my mouth - the feel, taste, smell - everything is right with the world when I'm allowed to suck him - and yes - I frequently think, "I love cock."

When I am serving with a sister slave and the Master is enjoying both of us, my perspective goes even more broadly. I am usually thinking, "I love this. I love his overflowing pleasure." I love nurturing and encouraging my sister slave as we work together. Serving together - whether we are serving the same man or serving individual men side by side or under a table - brings out the nurture in me and I feel us as one - her heart and my heart beating together, our lips working together. Slaves experience a sisterhood that is beautiful, sexual and strong.

I have lost two Doms because I don't have anal and I have never done it. Do you have it? Do you like it? Does it hurt like it looks? Is there a way to make it not hurt cause I might try it if I knew it didn't hurt.

───────────── ～ ─────────────

Thank you for trusting me with the question. I am sorry for your loss. It is always tough to lose what could be something good because of a limit.

The important thing is for you to decide if it is a soft limit (something you are willing to learn or change in time) or a hard limit (a never). If you "might try" - it sounds like this might be a soft limit. But - no matter where you are with the issue - the most important thing is to be honest with Doms about it. They have a right to know the truth and if anal sex is something they are not willing to do without - they have a right to leave.

Now: The answers to your question are: Yes, Yes, Yes, No-but.

1. Yes I have anal sex in which I am the receptive partner.

2. Yes, I do like it.

3. Yes, it hurts.

4. No, there is no way to make it painless - BUT there are things to do.

I think of anal sex a lot like piercing or tattooing - It hurts, it's worth it, and once you break the threshold and start doing it - you won't want to stop.

In anal sex the first part is the worst part. Then endorphins kick in and the pain becomes pleasurable. The painful part is the entry of the penis into your anal canal. There are 2 sphincters - the external (your anal orifice) and the internal (inside your body). Your Dom's penis must stretch open both sphincters and that is going to hurt. Your body isn't designed to "take in" through that orifice - it is designed to "push out" - so there will be resistance - that's actually one of the things that causes an intense feeling.

I don't find it excruciatingly painful — it's more uncomfortable than anything else. Kind of like an internal shiver. However, no one can tell you how much or little it may hurt you because every person has a different pain threshold. What will happen is that when your sphincters are open they will accommodate your Dom's cock and the pain will stop. Then, as he is sliding in and out, the feeling is intense and very pleasurable. It fills you in an intimate and energetic way. I view my body as a vessel for my Master and this is a way I love to receive him.

How can I learn to have anal sex? What steps can I take? My Master expects to use my ass and I'm scared.

―――――――――――――――――――――――――

Thanks for asking this question. Anal sex isn't one of those things anyone just "does naturally." In fact, the body isn't really designed to take things in anally so you will have to retrain your system, but that can add more pleasure to the process.

The best thing to do is start with a training butt plug. There are small sets that begin with a tapered thin plug and then build up to larger plugs. (Remember: Never use something anally that was not designed with a flared base for the anus, unless you like explaining these things in the emergency room). Tips:

1. Use a lot of lubrication at first. (The anus does not self-lubricate and the more lube you have in you the easier this becomes.) Those porn movies where guys just spit and start thrusting are ridiculous. Lots of lube.

2. Start small and tapered. Use a butt plug or your Dom's finger to begin with. Get used to the stretching and the "shiver" of pain that goes with opening the sphincters.

3. After you get used to entry, add some motion - either moving the plug back and forth or ask your Dom to do that with his finger (more lube!). That way - you can feel the good part as well (the anus is full of nerve endings and transmits pleasure as well as pain).

4. Keep building up until you decide you're ready for your Dom to take you anally. Be always honest and communicate. Most Doms want you to have a good experience and will work to slowly build up to this intimate moment.

If you decide anal sex is just not going to be for you - then let your Dom know that was your decision and work to find other ways he can enjoy and use your body. If it is a deal-breaker - then let him go, and find someone who is willing to experience all the gifts and joys you offer.

Does your Master put himself in your mouth after vaginal or anal sex?

Thanks for your question. It's always interesting what different people do and why.

No, my Master does not do any kind of contact after anal sex - either oral or vaginal. Neither one of us finds E.Coli or other feces related bacteria to be a turn on.

After vaginal use my Master will use my mouth - predominantly to clean him (and I dry him with my cheeks or hair or breasts). After anal I generally clean him with a warm wet soapy cloth, then kisses.

Porn pictures make that seem like it is a safe or okay thing to do, but it is simply putting the slave at risk for disease. It is better to stay healthy and play well.

Hi kate. I realize that consensual slavery is the life you've chosen, and you don't have scenes - just reality. Do certain moments or activities or types of serving turn you on more than others? Or are you just so deep into the mindset of pleasing that it doesn't matter how you feel about what you're doing when you're serving?

———————————— ∞ ————————————

Thanks for asking such a great question. Yes - there are things I <u>love, love, love</u> to do and things I don't really want to do, and even some things I dread doing. But, I do them all with as much passion and excellence as I can.

I have a very clear oral fixation so oral service delights me to no end. I love being spanked OTK, I prefer anal sex or sex from behind and I adore domestic service. I also love what I call "natural service" – If we go to the park or for a walk I will pack his lunch and serve him, etc. It's not big or sexy - but it's fun and I enjoy my service making his day more fun. A slave is also a companion. Any chance to meet those loves, thrills me.

I'm not really big on high pain sessions - so taking a single tail whipping, or breast cropping while clamped, Lexan ruler on my vulva, rimming, are some things that aren't high on my list. At that point I find comfort in the fact he's enjoying it and I do delve deep into that mindset to get me through.

I think every human has things they get turned on by more than others - the challenge is to make sure he gets the same kind of enthusiastic obedience whether it's something I enjoy or not.

Hey kate, what's your favorite way to take dick? Is there a way you won't let your Master fuck you?

———————⎯〰⎯———————

Thank you for asking this brutally clear question. Let me start with the second question first as it's easier. I am the property of my Master and he can use me in any way or position he chooses. I have never denied him any position or service he wanted.

I guess a list is easiest - here it is from favorite to least favorite (I'm sure there are lots of variations and other things to do, but these are the norm in my service).

1. Oral (always my favorite way to be taken).
2. Anal – all fours or face down/ass up.
3. Anal – Prone.
4. Vaginal – all fours or face down/ ass up.
5. Anal – bent at waist (like over a desk/couch/etc).
6. Vaginal bent at waist.
7. Mammary Intercourse (fun for a start but after a while this is very dull to me).
8. Vaginal Missionary (my least favorite, particularly if it is gentle. I'd much rather be "taken" or "used" than "made love to.")

Do you worship your Master's cock?

Thanks for that beautiful question. I do worship it. There is nothing better than to be allowed to spend gallons of time luxuriating it in every way possible.

Because I practice the Natural Order in my life, I view his cock as the scepter of his power. What gives him the superiority that allows me to consider him as someone I will consent to serve is his gender. Many women and men serve a female and find a lot of meaning there. However, for me, I have chosen to live a life where men are above me and where bowing down before their power is my natural inclination. My Master's cock is the emblem of that power and I get so much from focusing my devotion, attention and most especially, my mouth, on his member.

Cock worship is the natural by-product of a life lived in service of men.

How do you feel about men with small penises?
And large ones? Is penis size important to you?

———————————————————————

Truthfully, I adore all penises. They definitely make my mouth water.

I would say small to medium penises are more fun for me - because I have such an oral fetish. While I know many Masters love to hear a woman choking on their cock and that gagging sound arouses them - it is nice for me to be able to indulge a man's penis in my mouth, licking and sucking all the way to the balls without too much pushing against the back of my throat. I love to just lick and hold a penis (soft, hard, in-between) in my mouth.

Then, when a man with an average size penis decides to put his hand behind my head and fuck me in the face while his balls slap against me - there's still plenty to gag on, and that's fun too. (more so for him than me, admittedly.)

I've never had a Master with an overly long penis - I mostly see that in porn. In real life - most men in my life have been in the 4 to 8 inch category. I was given by my Master to a man with a very thick penis for a session. It was hell on the jaws, but very filling and stretching vaginally/anally so there are plusses and minuses to all sizes.

I guess - to me - every man is different (just like every woman) and all penises are to be lavished with luxurious attention whenever possible.

Do slaves prefer their Master to have a natural penis or a circumcised one?

————————— ∼ —————————

Thank you for asking. I love to serve all cocks, but my preference visually and sexually is circumcised. This is probably due to the fact that I am an American woman and it is the norm for men my age here in the US. Slaves from other countries where circumcision is rare probably prefer a natural penis. It is whatever you have been taught to expect that pleases most people.

It is important to remember that while a consensual slave worships the cock of her Master, she doesn't create relationship or consent to him based on his penis. It is his rituals, his attitude, and her ability to trust him that inspires a slave to consent to a man. Penis size, foreskin, or body components are all secondary to that.

When you are not with your Master, you are celibate, but what about the times you need a good spanking and he is not available? Self-spanking can be so arousing!

———————⌇——————

Thank you for this question. Spanking is so wonderful. Truth is - I lie awake at night craving spankings way more than I do sexual climax. In the beginning when he was just about being a maintenance Master, I could spank or punish myself - but I rarely did — it's just not as fun/meaningful.

When our roles grew stronger and I became his full property it was decided that would be against his wishes. I am his property and that means spanking myself for my pleasure is not within my right. So - when I am lucky enough to go serve him (particularly if we manage to squeeze extra time) - I am more than ready to beg him to beat my rear.

During the brief time I did not have a Master I did engage in self-spanking with a long handled wooden bath brush. It is very hard to hurt yourself enough to make a self-spanking worth it – but trust me – those overgrown hairbrushes can do the trick.

Dear kate: Do you like downtime? I find it very hard for young girls entering service. They need to be used and in downtime they feel lost, abandoned and bored. Some Doms habitually leave them in stress positions to fill the emptiness, and it is not a bad idea. What do you think?

———————— 〜 ————————

    I think all slaves are individuals and there are a lot of factors in helping them adjust or embrace the downtime. Ultimately, though, it all comes down to 1 word. Training.
    Age is a factor. I'm in my 40's. I grew up in a time when I had to wait for library books to be returned before I could read them. I grew up without a microwave. I spent my childhood waiting for hot dogs to actually <u>boil</u>. So – waiting and downtime isn't hard for me. But a young woman in our instant gratification culture - is going to need to learn to wait and that comes with training.
    The slave's personality is a factor - an introverted slave who enjoys reading and solitude will love downtime. An extrovert who wants to party or be the center of attention is going to struggle with the isolation and quiet in slavery.
    A wise Master won't just push them into a situation and say, "cope." A wise Master will bring the woman to her slavery through training, teaching, discipline, and re-training - step by step. Slaves are an investment, like a car, tool or property. Good Masters understand that.

What kind of enemas does your Master give you?
Are they simply for cleansing, or is an element of
pain (retention, cramping) part of his pleasure?
How are they for you?

———————————～————————————

    Thanks for asking about this personal practice.
Many Masters use enemas on their slaves but we don't talk
much about that. My Master uses soap and warm water
ones - for cleansing (particularly if an anal hook will be
involved) but also because he enjoys it. For me there is the
element of pain in the filling (and that weird sensation
when my body feels like it is expanding) and then he will
instruct me to hold it as long as I can take it - enjoying my
efforts to do so. He's not into the release - he will give me
permission then walk out of the room - advising me to
shower off and lay back over the bed when I'm ready for
whatever is next.
    They aren't my favorite thing (although, oddly, anal
temperature taking is something I enjoy) - but there is a
good feeling upon release and it's nice to know everything
is cleaned out and ready. I am also usually excited/nervous
because I know it means something great or painful is
going to happen.

You said you were straight but admit you do sex things with your Master's wife. So aren't you really Bi? Or do you just do it even though you hate it?

~

Thank you for this deep question. Please allow me to be very clear. Sexual orientation is not the same as sex acts.

Sexual orientation is the way a person sees, responds, and interacts in the world physically, emotionally, spiritually and sexually. It isn't about whom you have sex with. It is about the way you express yourself. Gay, Bisexual, Pan-sexual, Lesbian, Straight, etc. are all sexual orientations. My sexual orientation is heterosexual.

Sex acts are the things you do sexually. They have nothing to do with your sexual orientation. There is no better or worse to it - there is no gay or straight to it – it's a sex act.

When you combine the two (orientation and sex acts) - a woman's orientation toward women + kissing her breasts - you may get "lesbianism". Or a man's orientation to women + his penis in her vagina - you get heterosexuality. Both parts need to be together to create sexual identity.

So - to your question.

1. No, I do not identify as a bisexual. I am heterosexual.
2. Yes, I do sex acts with my Master's wife when he asks me or she asks me (he is my owner, she is his wife - she has a right to be served and respected as such).
3. No, I do not hate it. Slaves do things they don't necessarily enjoy - but this is not one of them. I enjoy her pleasure, the feel of her body, her softness and sweet smell,

and mostly the pleasure it gives my Master to see her have pleasure. I am thankful to serve her.

Do you allow yourself simple pleasures in life? Or
do you drive by things like the gourmet coffee
shop or the massage parlor thinking to yourself,
"slaves don't deserve such things" and not give
yourself a treat?

———————————— ∼ ————————————

Thank you for the question. I absolutely have
enjoyable things in my life. I love coffee, go to the spa, go
to movies, etc. I love my family and my life. Now, if my
Master said, "You aren't taking good care of your body and
I think you should go without dessert for two weeks." - I
would do it - but barring that kind of thing - my life is full.

Consensual slaves are human beings. We can't
forget that because when we do - no one has any fun.
Online Masters say stuff like, "You're just a hole for my
cock. A table for my drink, etc." It feels good to them, and
to women who enjoy being objectified. But it only feels
good because the woman is not really an object. If a man
said to a table, "You're a table," it wouldn't feel good -
because it is true and tables don't have feelings. But,
saying it to a person creates a demeaning/reducing
environment that feels good.

As a slave, the joy I feel when a man says, "You're
a set of holes made for a cock" is the ability to accept that,
to endure it, and for that moment to know it's true and my
holes will be used for his pleasure. My human being-ness is
part of my slavery.

Many Masters can indulge a slave with good things.
Slaves don't "deserve" anything. But they can receive good
as well as harsh gifts, as well as pain when the Master
chooses. It is never that a slave deserves. It is always that a
Master gives. A slave should be grateful for those things.

One of the joys of accepting my slavery is that I live a life every day where I am grateful - and a life of thankfulness is a really happy one.

Is orgasm denial something your Master uses with you often? I cannot imagine serving without being able to orgasm (obviously with permission).

―――――――――――――――

Orgasm denial is pretty much a part of a slave's life. You aren't allowed to touch yourself - and a lot of the sex is anal, oral or quick vaginal (because the build up through foreplay is intense) so learning to live without focusing on your own release all the time is a must. And trust me - when release is allowed - it is amazing, and worth it.

Many new couples to D/s or M/s spend way too much time focusing on orgasm, however. The point is to create a relationship of trust, placement and service. When you spend all your time online or together worried about when someone is going to come, how long it has been since someone came, or edging and orgasm control – you aren't developing the real relationship. Eventually, even the most amazing orgasms are just a few moments and you have to deal with the rest of the night. Orgasm and orgasm denial are great training tools and sexual moments, but there simply is more to life.

I'm assuming your Master does not always want you to have sexual release during the session, and that your pleasure was entirely about his pleasure. Does he make you ask permission to come? Does he let you know what a good girl you are?

─────────────────∿─────────────────

Thank you for your lovely comment and question. My pleasure/climax is not something he is usually concerned about, although he is generous with the stimuli to cause them. I did climax underneath him before he withdrew, but I was in a great deal of pain and it was a small one.

We are not a very "orgasm centered" relationship. I see a lot of Tumblr couples where the sub/slave's orgasm is this huge deal - whether she is allowed one, or denying her one, having her beg to climax, etc. For us - my Master really couldn't care less if I climax or not - as long as he is satisfied and gets release. It's just not a focus for him and he feels having me "ask permission" and focusing on whether or not I can come just breaks his concentration for what he is doing. So - if I release while he is using me - he enjoys it. If I don't - he's okay with that, and I accept it as the reality of an owned woman.

For the most part - we don't spend gallons of time obsessing on that one little part of our whole relationship. Let's face it - if slavery were just about getting the "right to orgasm or having an orgasm" - I could do that on my own or with a lover who was much less demanding. Our purpose is service (for me) and obedience/power (for him). The rest are just the fun sidebars to a great situation.

As to being a "good girl" - he wouldn't use that phrase because it doesn't really fit us - but he does let me know when he has enjoyed my body, or what he enjoys

about my service. He values me and appreciates my
consent and efforts. So I am affirmed and assured often.

Hi, kate. I'm a big fan of your blog and have a question. I notice in BDSM porn that a Dom will often order a female subject to ask permission before she has an orgasm. And the subject will gasp and fight and seem to hold off the climax internally- until given permission to cum and then just explode in ecstasy. Is this even possible? Can a female mentally resist an escalating orgasm if they have no control over the stimulation?

Thank you so much for the lovely compliment about my blog. As to your question – it's the age old answer – porn, like reality TV and other exaggerated efforts, is entertaining – but not real – and the things that are real in porn aren't healthy.

The science of female orgasm is pretty simple. The majority of sex actually occurs in the brain. Stimulation creates impulses that go up the nerve endings to the brain. Initially the brain responds to arousal by lubricating the body and swelling the area. Then, the brain responds to increasing stimuli by tightening the muscles and releasing a small amount of adrenaline to increase energy (why women get red/flushed during sex). The more muscles involved (the pelvic floor, hips, legs, etc.) the larger the orgasm. The brain speeds up the heart/breathing – (essentially getting your body ready to fight). After a while, the brain realizes tightening and shaking the muscles isn't helping and the stimuli are still occurring. Pressure is building. At some point (at the maximum amount of stimuli the brain can take) it releases chemicals to release the muscles – including dopamine, serotonin, and muscle relaxants to allow the body to get away. The point when the brain releases the chemicals and the muscles release is orgasm. That easy. It's a basic fight/flight response.

So – a woman can "distract" her brain for a bit, thinking about non-sexual things or using her mind to reduce the stimulation – but inevitably the brain is going to decide it's time and release. There is a little women can do to hold off for a time – but not a tremendous amount.

Many porn actresses take drugs that limit and slow down the brain's reaction – so their body endures much more – and then the "overflowing release" is just acting. You know those pics that get revered online where people say, "look at the faraway look in her eyes – she's in 'subspace'." Actually, she's just drugged up.

The point of porn is to start the stimuli to get the brain to release the chemicals. It's fantasy, not a documentary.

My Master says if I touch myself without permission he will punish me with forced orgasms. Is that even possible? How can you punish someone with pleasure? Has that ever happened to you? What's it like?

―――――――――――〜――/――――――――――

Thank you for this wonderfully honest question. Please believe me when I tell you that being punished with forced orgasms is one of the most painful, unpleasant things that can happen to you and you don't want to flirt with that possibility. Obey your Master.

I have been punished with forced orgasms about four times in my whole twenty-year history of being a spanked girlfriend/sub/slave and I hated each and every one of them. The level of pain and exhaustion I felt during, and the entire chemical and physical depletion I felt afterward was really a bad feeling. I truly knew I had been punished severely.

Every Master does things a little differently but the basics of being punished with forced orgasms is like this: The slave is physically restrained with hands tied down and legs restrained open (such as with a spreader bar secured to the bed or floor bolts). You essentially cannot move either your hands or legs. You can't get away or act to stop anything. Then the Master applies a very strong vibrator like a Hitachi wand directly on your vulva right above your clitoris so that your very sensitive clit takes the bulk of the 6,000 RPM vibration.

Very quickly your muscles tighten, causing you to pull against your bonds, then you release in a huge full climax that causes your hips to bounce up and down and your body to absorb the waves of your release. In normal orgasms, you'd experience those pleasant waves, the stimulation would stop and you would curl up in your

Master's arms and fall asleep. In the case of forced orgasm, the stimulus isn't removed. The wand is still whirring, pummeling your over-sensitive, swollen clit underneath it as the nerves send pain signals to the brain.

Soon you are trying to jerk, move or pull your hands out of the restraint just to stop the painful pressure on core as your clit tightens once more and a second rubbery orgasm happens...and it just keeps going... The orgasms aren't even pleasurable anymore. They just hurt and you try do anything you can to stop them. Eventually between the burning, swollen ache of your midsection and the physical exhaustion of trying to pull or move your body to get away from the sensation, you just become a sobbing, begging, hurting being.

The worst part, besides the fatigue and muscle soreness, is that the next day or so you feel completely at a loss to cope with anything. Your brain has released so many chemicals to help you endure your orgasms that you end up just feeling numb in the head.

Giving you a couple of orgasms and then aftercare is something a generous Master does. Punishing you with repeated forced orgasms – is pure sadistic punishment. Avoid it, if possible.

I was intrigued by your answer recently that you can take 12 strokes of the cane without restraint. It makes me wonder how "tough" a woman are you? Have you ever had the single tail whip? Ever been strapped across the breasts or genitals? Is there some level of pride in taking what punishment your Master chooses to give you?

———————————————～～————————————

     Thank you for your questions. I am honored you wrote to me. Yes, I have been whipped with the single tail whip, although not in 2 years. My previous Master was fond of it for training purposes. I was not. But I did endure and found that ice baths (10 minutes) help with the swelling/stiffness, and later emulsifying milk baths (warm) help repair the skin.

     Yes, I have been strapped, and cropped across my breasts and vulva. My current Master enjoys cropping the vulva as a form of foreplay.

     "Tough" is a hard word to accurately define - what is "tough" to one person may not seem "tough" to another. There are also different arenas of "toughness" so I'll give you a list of things I can do and you can decide my "toughness" as you please.

     I personally think all women who bow before a man and offer him her body and will are in some way "tough." Submission is an act of strength, not weakness.

     Mentally, I am able to submit to any command regardless of how much pain, bodily fluids, or endurance it may require. I am also disciplined in keeping silent, and keeping my thoughts inside, unless requested. I have a strong will and mind.

     Physically my pain threshold is medium to high-ish. I enjoy pain up to a medium level (I like minor cuts, bruising, welts. I prefer instruments that sting as opposed to thud). My limit on painful events is permanent scarring, flowing blood loss (drawing blood on the skin is fine - like with a switch or single tail - creating a deep enough wound that blood collects and flows (like a gushing nose, or deep wound is not okay), dizziness (vasovagal response) or loss of consciousness. I'm in my 40's, so I'm not as strong as I used to be - but still stronger than many for at least a little while.

I ache, bleed, gasp, and cry out like any other woman would. But, at the end of the session, I do remember to say "Thank You."

You said riding the wooden pony was the most painful thing you have ever done. Can you describe your experience with the pony? Was it almost too much? How long did you ride? Was it an earned punishment or a test? It looks extremely hard to handle. I've had a very tight crotch rope - is the pony similar?

The pony belonged to a Master friend of my Master at the time - The ride was a "challenge" - to see if I could do it and how I would act if I couldn't. My Master was looking for things that really pushed me. His friend suggested the pony.

I was supposed to ride for an hour. I made it 43 minutes and 36 seconds the first time. 15 minutes the second (2 months later). It took me nearly 4 days to walk properly again. I have done small things with a crotch rope - it's similar - but the wood is so much denser the pain lasts a lot longer to me. And - one person's pain isn't the same as another's -so you may have suffered as much on a crotch rope.

It is not "almost too much" - it is way too much for me. The pony I rode was a saw horse-like apparatus with a cross plank sanded to a dull point (not sharp but a definite triangle, which is a little different from the flat wooden ones.

It looks deceptively easy. I started naked with hand/ankle cuffs, my hands bound behind my back and my feet on blocks. I felt it pressing against my vulva (the wood spreads your labia open almost immediately), then he clipped my ankles to the back legs of the horse so my full body weight was resting on my vulva. It was uncomfortable, but not bad at first…then it built like a fire - I began to feel achy and tried to find a better position.

I would move my body forward then that would throb, so I'd move backward and my perineum would throb, then the sides would ache - the more I moved I would get a few seconds of relief then the new spot would hurt more. From my Master's position it looked like I was trying to screw the pony, which added to the humiliation. (By the end, he and the other Master were teasing me saying things like,"fuck that horse" and "ride that pony" - but I was in too much pain to really care.)

I didn't realize until I experienced it myself that rocking to relieve the pain is exactly why they call it riding the pony. The pain went from ache to burn to sharp brutal cramps. I was crying, screaming, snot running down my face, practically barking, promising anything, everything, to get through this… just moving back and forth trying to escape the pain. My Master realized I wasn't going to make it and moved closer to me. Finally, I said, "I'm passing out" and he held me while the other released me and put blocks under my feet.

The sharpness released as soon as I stood (with their help) and got off. But you know that painful, throbbing, stingy feeling your feet get when they fall asleep and you put the circulation back? Imagine that in your genitals- for hours afterward. I was bruised back and forth, and ached for days.

The second try I was entirely mentally blocked from the first attempt. The moment the pain set in I was done. Every time I got off that thing I swore- never again. I meant it. But, if my current Master said, "You are going to ride the pony today." - I would disrobe and attempt to do it. That's consensual slavery – it's not always about what you want. Sometimes it's about what you have to do.

I fear this seems like a shallow question on some level. I promise it is not! Do you like the "pain" and all the rough stuff? I presume hard anal and other things can hurt. Or is it just part of the servitude lifestyle which you feel you were born for? Do you physically enjoy the actual acts, right there, right then? Or is it knowing it's part of the bigger picture of what you do?

Thank you for the great questions. They are not shallow at all - but valid questions on many levels. I enjoy the pain when I have it, the memory of how I got it and the slight soreness that lasts a day or two after (that's kinda the best part).

I have a medium to high pain threshold and enjoy the sensation of stinging pain (canes, light cords, light belts/crops) more than thud pain (paddles, heavy straps, etc.). However, I get a feeling of pleasure from most mid-level pain with a connective sexual purpose (so - I don't get excited when I have a headache or fall down stairs - but sexual pain, punishment pain - yes I enjoy it.)

The part I don't enjoy is when it goes over the top of my threshold and I experience the fight/flight mechanism or I fear I am going to have to stop the session because of it. Recently I had a vasovagal reaction during a session and had to stop for 30 minutes to get over the nausea, which didn't bother the Master, but bothered me. Then we started back and all was well.

Anal sex only hurts in the beginning for me - once he is past the second sphincter and thrusting in and out - it feels divine. So, I agree it's largely both – I enjoy the pain, and I enjoy the relationship in which I feel safe and free to experience it.

Does your Master use intense sensations (pain)
while you service him sexually, or do you service
him without any added sensation? My Master is
slowly getting me to accept more pain during
sexual service because he believes the only
pleasure I should feel is from giving him pleasure.
He is also introducing humiliation - does your
Master do that too?

Thanks for asking. Pain is sometimes a part of my
sexual service, either because it gives him pleasure to see
me serve through pain, or sometimes because he knows I
get a certain amount of pleasure from pain. He may be in a
generous mood and give me pleasure as well.

Physical pain is a tricky thing. Remember — sex
happens in the brain. After you go through pain and sex
together for awhile, your brain begins to associate sexual
pleasure with pain (it's called the Pleasure/Pain Principle) -
Now - sharp or uninvited pain won't seem sexual — but
spanking, breast clamps, welts, etc. will begin to make you
aroused and wet once your brain begins to associate those
sensations with the feelings of sexual use and pleasure.

Sharp/intense pain can have the opposite effect (the
brain will add more adrenaline and less dopamine to your
system so you will become more edgy, have a harder time
focusing on anything (including your Master), and have an
increased desire to run or fight.

The best way for your Master to know which
reaction creates the best combination for his pleasure is to
start with lower levels of pain and increase over time,
noting the reaction and holding listening sessions where
you can describe your sensations. As far as making his

pleasure your "only" pleasure - that's likely to backfire.
One can only jerk the brain around so much - then it starts
doing things on its own.

Slaves aren't really prone to humiliation producing
a reaction. Because - we are slaves - as long as we follow a
Master's commands - we are happy and aroused by what
we do because we are obeying. So we don't feel shame
(because a good slave is focused on what the Master thinks,
not what others think) and so humiliation kinda falls flat.
I've done things that would be embarrassing if my Master
hadn't commanded it - but they never hold a significant
interest or reaction.

Have you ever served a Master who enjoyed humiliating you? It's an interest of mine and I'd love to hear some of your experiences in that regard. Your description of having your mouth washed out with soap was quite hot for me (probably less so for you).

───────────────✵───────────────

Thanks for this honest question, (And, yes - you are probably enjoying my mouth being washed out far more than I did).

Humiliation is different when you are a consensual slave. I don't feel the pain of humiliation as long as I am serving my Master - so instead of it being the kind of humiliation where I say, "Oh, I'm so embarrassed someone is seeing this." It's more the kind that says, "Here I am, a grown woman standing in the corner with a bar of soap in my mouth because I don't watch my mouth." I'm so embarrassed I let my Master down.

I've been put in humiliating-ish situations - exposed in a hotel room to the room service clerk, wearing a collar out of town in shops and restaurants, giving head with limited time before someone comes by and sees us, taken over the hood of a car where adults could see, fetching a switch at a truck stop in front of others, etc. But I didn't feel shame about them. I did as I was told. But I also secretly hoped too many people wouldn't see. So, there's a normal sense of human shame there.

When my current Master decides to discipline me (as opposed to spanking/whipping for his pleasure) he will say humiliating things such as, "Look at you, being punished for doing so and so…" and that does shame me. There are also the contemplative humiliations - writing lines, corner time, fetching a switch…and those can be very powerful as well.

Have you ever been punished by someone who was genuinely angry at you at the time? I want to know what it is like to volunteer yourself to be bound- truly helpless- and then be punished beyond your limits.

Punished by someone genuinely angry? As an adult - no. A wise Master understands that for the slave to give up control - he MUST be in control. It is consensual slavery. You have to remember - almost all of these "slap-a-slut" rants you see online are fantasy, built on pictures from porn. They are designed for entertainment/arousal/masturbation. Most Dom/sub or Master/slave relationships aren't just one long ugly fuckpig rally where you get spit on, slapped and assaulted by an angry acting man all day every day. At best - those kinds of things happen as a session or kinky night and are enjoyed by both. Most couples who really live in this reality - it's a very well communicated, controlled life and Masters who intend to have their slave for more than 2 hours realize acting out true anger is a bad idea. Besides, most Masters have a bit of sadism in them. They don't have to be mad to hurt you - they can do it with a smile on their face.

As for what it is like to be bound and punished past your limit - it is different in every person - largely because every person is different and has a unique level of pain tolerance, resistance and response.

I remember very well the first time I got spanked past what I thought I could take as an adult. I was full of cranky attitude and my boyfriend at the time decided I needed to release tension. He bound my hands, put me over his lap, took a wooden hairbrush and small leather strap and beat my rear. At first I enjoyed it, eventually I started kicking and squirming, then the spanking dance was in full force and I told him I had enough. He said to trust him. As my rear went past boiling, "fight or flight" kicked in and I started bucking and squirming (flight) and trying to kick him (fight). He locked my legs down between his and kept on spanking, I felt like I was going crazy for a moment — then started screaming which lead to sobbing, deep brutal exhausting sobbing — and my tension and muscles released. It wasn't pretty like the pictures appear - I was a sweating, drippy-snotty, entirely bruised and swollen wreck. But I felt 100% better. I slept on my stomach for a few days - but I slept really well.

That's pretty much the process on a physical level. After a while your fight/flight instinct kicks in and you are full of adrenaline (it sometimes can upset your stomach), then when that doesn't help, you just lose control - muscles pull, sobs happen, then your brain tries to ease the situation by shoveling serotonin into your system to at least lessen your anxiety - and you get the momentary floaty feeling - like a athletic high – it's fleeting but it feels great.

The key to all of it is a Master or Dom you trust. Without trust, your brain will lock up, you won't get those handy brain chemicals and it will be a miserable experience. It isn't something to try until you know each other really well and have made a plan in advance as to why you're doing it, and how it will work.

The Master's truth is: "I will hurt you but not harm you." - If you don't believe that 100% about the man who is going to do this to you - wait until you do.

How often is it necessary for your Master to punish you for disciplinary reasons? How do those punishments differ from those administered for fun?

⎯⎯⎯⎯⎯⎯⎯⎯⎯〜⎯⎯⎯⎯⎯⎯⎯

Thank you for these questions.
Discipline/punishment is always an interesting topic. I am not punished (disciplined) regularly. In fact it is very rare and almost always I have asked for it. Reasons:

1. Slavery is different from submission. With submission - there usually has to be a reason or need for a Master to give a severe or punishing whipping. In slavery - there is no reason - you're a slave - that's the reason. So - slave owners don't have to 'nitpick' or find excuses to whip you really hard - they more or less just let you serve and do what they want.

2. I do what I am expected and I live the way I have chosen. There is no need to punish me. Sometimes a man will email me a sexual scenario then ask if I "broke my chastity" and have to report to my Master (hoping they caused me to do some naughty thing). The answer is always no. If I couldn't keep control of myself - I wouldn't be online. A good slave is a disciplined one, not one looking for trouble.

3. When I am disciplined it is usually because I have told my Master about losing my temper at work or acting badly. I want him to punish me because that is not the kind of woman I want to be.

Punishment sessions are very different. He asks me to schedule them on different days than my usual service. He doesn't feel he should lose out on pleasure because I am being punished. On punishment session day I arrive, strip, wait in the slave quarters on my knees hands behind head, eyes down. He lectures me, shaming me for what I should rightfully be ashamed of. Then I ask him to punish me. I take the position he commands, and take the punishment (sharp, harsh, painful) he decides upon until we are both convinced I have paid for my issue (no warm up, no breaks, no mercy rubbing - just fast, brutal, corrective).

Then - the really bad part. He will make me kneel on the floor legs wide open, hands open, no gag for comfort - in silence - my body stinging from the pain. He will read, check his mail, etc., then open his pants, and stroke his penis while I am forced to watch - wanting it in every part of my body. Knowing I need it to comfort my pain, knowing I want it in my mouth to appease him, to drain the pleasure back into my body from him. He will stroke himself until he climaxes, watching me watch him knowing I am desperate for his cock. Then he will say "You're dismissed, kate." And only that - making me leave in silence, empty, wanting, and in chastity until he sees me again.

Trust me – it's very effective. I usually hand-write a letter to him that night. That provides closure. When I show up for my regular session - all is past and we are ready for me to enjoy and honor him as he pleases.

To me, punishment isn't something I seek or want. It is sometimes what I deserve and endure.

I am truly fascinated by your blog. Love to hear the mindset of a true slave woman. You just posted you sometimes take 12 of the best with the cane. Does your Master restrain you for your caning, or can you take it without being bound?

———————————～——————————

Thank you for the lovely compliment. I am always happy to know others achieve arousal or happiness in the sharing of ideas.

I am not restrained for caning. I am expected to take it and be thankful for it. I generally am placed over the bed and I grip the coverlet for support through the pain. If I were to move away or attempt to escape the cane - I am sure I would be getting a lot more than 12.

Restraining a slave is usually for when you are going to punish her – with extreme pain or forced orgasms. I normally get the cane for his pleasure and that does not require me to be tied down. In fact, the site of a slave forcing herself to take the pain without the help of a restraint is often what arouses the Master more than the strokes themselves.

Do you think it is acceptable for a servant to initiate, suggest, or request punishment? For example, is it okay to tell your Owner, "I really feel like I need a good spanking and some time in the corner." Or is this completely out of line?

———————————〜———————————

Thank you for the question. I think it is easy to give our Masters god-like status in our minds because we subscribe to them so much authority, ability, and power. But, the reality is - Masters are people. They get tired. They get busy. And, sometimes they fail to see something even if it is right in front of them.

To me it is a slave's duty - within established protocol - to let the Master know if the slave has a need. Don't make the Master read your mind, that's lazy. You serve the Master, not the other way around. A Master can always say, "No, not today." The Master may also decide you need more than a spanking and give you more than you bargained for. That's the Master's choice. But, if you don't ask, the Master can't know.

More couples (vanilla and fetish) break apart because of the things they don't say - rather than the things they do. Besides, a really good spanking sounds delicious right now. Mmmm

You have a discipline session every other week. Does it leave marks? I had to do some hasty (vanilla) explaining at the gym when my still-welted butt was spotted by some friends. Do you explain why your butt/thighs are marked or bruised?

―――――――――~――――――

There's nothing more uncomfortable than explaining the normal wear and tear of everyday submission to a vanilla person. Depending on the situation, I handle it any number of ways (Yes, my discipline leaves deep and lasting welts - it wouldn't be discipline if it didn't).

If it's someone who knows me from work (where they think I am very serious and frigid) I'll act like I'm joking and say, "You know, when I'm not here I am a seriously kinky person and it's from a whip after someone put a large metal hook in my bottom." They just wave their hands, laugh and walk off. No one would ever believe the truth of that statement.

If it's a family member or friend who may be worried I am being abused or harmed - I have told them, "This isn't something I want to share. It's private. But, you need to know there is not a mark on me that I didn't ask for or want." They accept that.

I have found the more you accept it the easier it is for others to accept it. My esthetician at the spa asked me some questions in the beginning, but now just works with it like it's just another challenge to my skin.

If it is some stranger (like at the gym) I don't explain it. It's like people who put pictures of their dinner on facebook - the truth is - not everyone needs to know - and most people don't care.

Do you do anything to reduce the pain and swelling of your Master's discipline? Seventeen with the cane on your inner thighs, gagged, plugged and restrained is certainly "generous" of your Master. What a beautiful slave.

———————————～———————————

Thanks so much for your question and lovely compliment. Friday was indeed a rough and generous adventure. They aren't always that challenging but I am lucky to be given a chance to embrace such things.

I do engage in a number of healing techniques. I use an elemental milk bath either in a warm bath or directly on the skin for its rejuvenating power. If the skin is not broken I often use mineral ice to promote better circulation (speeds healing for bruises) and if the skin is broken I use Neosporin to prevent infection and for skin repair. I also cover open wounds in liquid skin – which seals the wound. Ibuprofen for a few days also reduces swelling quite well.

Today the biggest challenge was just sitting with my legs pressed together in a lady-like fashion. My older sister noticed my distinctly sore walk when she dropped the girls off this morning (she knows what I do) and was teasing me saying, "Been riding a horse?" and "I think your marble just turned into a soccer ball." (Our mother used to tell us we should always sit "as though we were holding a marble between our knees," i.e. legs together – and it's a huge joke in our family).

Pretty much – the more you care for your body beforehand – (exercise, skin care, stretching) the better for the healing afterward.

I love that you give yourself aftercare instead of relying on your Master to baby you. Has that always been the case, even when you were married to your Master?

———————～——————

Thank you for the affirmation and question. I have pretty much always done my own aftercare - largely by choice and desire to do so. I am not a cuddle and soothe kind of person. I remember in graduate school I met a guy who was interested in spanking. On our first real date/conversation he said, "I want to spank you really hard and then I will hold and comfort you, rubbing lotion on you and making you feel better." I thought, "That sounds awful." We never had a second date. I am not big on the "after care, dry her tears, hold and comfort" thing. I'm more into, "We're done here, bye." That way I can enjoy the pain, the pleasure and the calm afterglow all by myself.

For some submissives and slaves, aftercare by their Master is one of the main reasons they do this. They like being held, having tears kissed away and the attention and cuddling. So, for a woman who needs nurturing, having a Master do aftercare is very important, but it's not for me and I'm happy to leave that for others.

Serving a Couple

The Slave Speaks

The first question someone usually asks me is, "How did you decide you wanted to serve a married couple?" The answer is, "I didn't." I thought I was going to serve a married man whose wife knew what he was doing and wanted no part in it. Serving them as a couple evolved over time in a very natural, easy-going way and I think that's what makes it all work. It's the first piece of advice I give every consensual slave who wants to serve a couple: Remember, their relationship comes first and is the basis of everything else.

My Master and the Lady have a beautiful marriage. They share and work together well. They have raised children together, pursued dreams together, and endured the joys and hardships that life has to offer. They are very alike except for one thing: She's vanilla, and he's not. At some point in their marriage he told her he didn't want to have an affair, but he needed more sexually and personally than she was willing to offer. He needed to be a Dominant in every sense of the word. She told him to pursue his needs, but – she didn't want to see, hear or know about what he did. The separation worked for many years, with a few notable disasters along the way, then I came along.

At first, we would meet at his house and he would spank and use me, then I would clean up and leave long before she came home. One day, she came home early. I greeted her politely, and left as quickly as possible. She started asking questions about me. Then, one day she left the Master a note asking if he could have me polish their silver and iron some linens. I happily obliged. She began leaving more notes, eventually allowing me to make dinner for them and serve them. The more domestic service she allowed, the happier we all were. In time, she got used to me, felt secure with me, and decided I was a plus to their marriage.

Over the course of the first two years we went from strangers to Lady and slave. I have tremendous respect for the Lady. She allows another woman to sexually satisfy her husband and to serve her sexual needs as well. She willingly reveals her intimate moments in my arms, and allows me to thank her for the pleasure. I think it takes a lot of courage, and love, to make the decisions she has made. I honor her for that.

Serving a couple means more work, more attentiveness, and more pleasure. Her happiness makes him happy. His happiness makes me happy. So we are all in this together. There are things to remember:

- *She is his love, and I am his slave.*
- *The goal is to make their relationship better, never challenge it.*
- *Her needs are his needs and must be met.*
- *She is the wife of my owner and is entitled to anything she asks within my consent to my owner.*
- *I should never draw his attention toward myself. When they are together, he should look at her.*

We have evolved into a joyous, successful triad. I still see my Master for one-to-one sessions full of pain, sex and service. But I also rejoice in the moments with the two of them – cooking, cleaning, serving them at a festival or event, or even just walking in the woods behind them. I am profoundly grateful they have let me into their home, their life, and their bed.

I'm thinking of serving a Dom couple. Do you have any tips and or advice for me? Is it something you'd recommend over serving a single Dom?

―――――――――――――――

Thanks for your question. I am honored that you seek my opinion. Serving a couple is very different than serving a single Dom in terms of focus and intention. Things to remember:

1. Have a distinct time for training and listening sessions to establish clear communication. If both of the members of the couple are Dominant it can happen that they both give tasks or overwhelm you with decisions. The hope is they work together to Dom you – but – ask them up front what the protocol is when there are conflicting/competing moments. In my case, my Master's wife is not a Dom- however, he told me, "Anything she wants comes first. If you're serving me and she asks for something stop and do it. Don't look to me – just do it." So – clear training and communication is important.

2. Accept there is a different focus. When you serve a single Dom, even it is not a romantic relationship, you are the focus at the moment and the Dom's whole attention is on you and your service. When you serve a couple, you are not the focus of the service. The couple pays attention to each other and derives pleasure together using you. That doesn't mean you won't get attention but it is a different feeling because the attention is spread out among the group. It also means when you aren't serving - they have their own life, love, and patterns. You have to have a strong self and personal life to serve a couple.

3. Be sure about what you want from this. If you are looking for training, or a place to serve that is enjoyable and challenging for a time, serving a couple is fantastic. However, if you are young or looking for a long term/life

relationship – you need to be aware that serving a couple is not likely to offer that. Couples are locked into each other. They change, they grow, they have kids or they move – and they make their decisions based on what is best for their relationship (rightfully so), not what is best for you. That doesn't mean they are not committed to you – but the commitment is based on their unit of being, not your needs. So if you are looking for a life partner/long-term scenario you might do better with a Dom.

3 Nevers When Serving A Couple:

- Never play one against the other to get what you want.
- Never become the communicator between them ("he said you would…" or "he told me to tell you that…").
- Never purposely draw one's attention away from the other or set up any kind of "competition" environment. You are to support them as a unit - never divide them.

Serving a couple is tremendously fun and very exhausting. Think of the energy it takes to please one person – now multiply it by two. It's like being part of the family. At the same time – it is not the same as having a family of your own.

Dear kate, When did your relationship to your Master change from "discipline Master" to being owned by him? Was there a ceremony to mark the transition? Your words yesterday about why you are grateful to him were really moving.

———————————— ～ ————————————

Thank you for this great clarifying question - our way of defining our relationship has changed since I started this blog - but the relationship itself has evolved much more slowly and not changed as much.

In May it will be 3 years since my former Master announced he was moving and gave me (with my consent) to Master Daniel. We did training together with my former Master. As a ritual - I started training with my current Master by giving him the key to my chastity belt, and when training was over - 3 months later - he transitioned me from a training collar to my current collar. That was also the last day I saw or heard from my former Master.

I am very busy with a lot of commitments. So, I told my Master I couldn't really be a slave and serve him with the kind of devotion or constant presence a slave should. He said to think of him as a "Maintenance Master" - someone to spank and sexually use me on an appointment basis until my life changed and I could serve more deeply. At the time - his wife (vanilla) knew he had subs/slaves but didn't want to know anything about them or the process. So - all appointments would be at his home while she was out.

My Master was patient and wise. He allowed his wife to change in her own time, and allowed me the comfort of thinking this was "maintenance only" (so I wouldn't fret over my competing responsibilities) thus the change happened in a natural way.

Over time, his wife met me, started asking him to assign me tasks/chores - and would see me still finishing her tasks (ironing, polishing silver) when she got home. She allowed me to make dinner for them, and also started talking to me. We discovered we have many non-kink things in common. I started serving them at social settings and more frequently. Eventually she told my Master it would be okay to invite me to their bed on rare occasion. So - <u>her</u> transition really propelled our transition as Master and slave.

On Jan. 1, I served my Master and his wife for New Year's. The Master told me they were both so very happy with my service and the changes it made in their life. Since it was clear my life/time/commitments were not going to change, and they were too busy for much more than we already had - my Master wanted us to make the arrangement full and permanent and just be my owner/Master - not my "Maintenance Master." His wife held my hand and said, "I don't want this to change. We don't want to lose you," and she kissed my cheek. That was the closest thing to ritual we had for that transition and I cherish that moment more than any "thing" (collar, ring, etc.) they could give me.

I'm incredibly curious about your Master and his wife. Is she his sub or slave too? What is your relationship to her? Do you sexually service each where they can see one another, or do you service each privately?

Thanks for your questions. My Master and his wife have been married a very long time. She is vanilla; he is not. She doesn't want to participate in kink for herself, but doesn't mind its presence in his life. They decided many years ago to open their marriage for him to express his natural desires to dominate and own women. I am not the first slave he has owned and he only owns one at a time because he has duties to his family, job, etc.

Our situations matched perfectly – he needed a part-time slave who understood it was service and not a love relationship per se, and I needed to serve but have no time for a full-time relationship. He was a friend of my Master who moved, so I already knew him. We did training with my Master before he moved so it was a very smooth transition.

My service sessions are done when she is not at home (she is aware of them), and part of my service is to clean up everything and ensure the house looks the same as it did before I arrived so she is never bothered or inconvenienced. They have a service quarters bedroom (where the toys/implements, etc. are kept as well) so I am never used on her bed without her consent.

We are all friendly and I always treat her with the same amount of respect I treat him. I see her as a free woman, and the female owner of the house where I serve. She understands I am their slave. She does enjoy a fun evening or time of service occasionally, but most of the things she wants are domestic service oriented things. I draw her a bath and wash her back or wash her hair. I iron and lay out her clothes and help dress her. If it's just a night at home I make them popcorn and kneel by his chair but refresh her drink or give her a shoulder massage.

If I am with them together sometimes he will want a sexual service (usually oral) and I will perform that for him in her presence and it doesn't bother her. Sometimes, after a dinner or ballet or something we've attended, they may want me to accompany them to bed for service – usually oral service on both of them to start them off – then I'm dismissed or sometimes I will hold her as he makes love to her or we will both stimulate him. It's a very comfortable arrangement between three adult people.

The trick about serving a man when his wife is present is to always remember it's about her and him, not you. Never argue, correct, or suggest anything to her. Never dress nicer than she does (I have a series of plain black dresses and low heels when I accompany them), or draw more attention than she does, and NEVER do anything that would draw his attention off of her and onto you. She is his wife. I am his servant.

I know I seem obsessed with the idea you serve
your Masters wife sometimes but - is there
anything she makes you do that you don't like?
What is your favorite thing to do with her?

———————————⌇————————————

Thank you for your questions. I imagine you are
curious because it is either a situation you desire, or one
you've never seen. Either way, sharing our experiences
makes us all stronger.

All slaves do things they don't like. It is part of
consensual slavery. But, I've never been told to do
anything sexually for her that I didn't want to do. She's not
a very sexual person. She particularly enjoys having
domestic service done, so sometimes when we are having
an evening of service she will ask me to iron something, or
fold her laundry or something her maid forgot to do. I don't
like folding laundry (even my own), but I do it and thank
her for it. And, there is still the excitement of being
collared, naked, and standing at the ironing board where
my Master can see me doing chores. Usually the only thing
I feel, even when I'm scrubbing their kitchen floor on my
hands and knees (with a plug in my rear) for her - is
gratitude.

My favorite thing to do is hold her while my Master
makes love to her. Their sex is very different from his
usage of me, and I enjoy seeing that side of him. He goes
very slowly, gently and lovingly with her. I usually lay at
her side with my arm around her, nuzzling her neck, giving
her small kisses, or whispering things like "you are so
beautiful" in her ear. Then I get the honor of holding her
through her climax - feeling her body tighten move as she
gasps. It's a priceless intimate moment.

Hi kate - First, you have a wonderful blog and as a Dom I enjoy reading about your service. I enjoy hearing about your thoughts and feelings as much as your activity. In another posting you said you enjoyed holding your Master's wife while she orgasms. I would like to hear more about that, how you feel, etc. Also, do you ever clean her after they have sex?

———————————————

Thank you so much, Sir, for your lovely compliment and affirmation. I value your time to tell me that.

When I am called to their bed to serve them both, I usually begin by preparing her and using my mouth to get her very close to orgasm then I wrap my arms around her (spoon style), kiss, nuzzle and whisper sweet thoughts in her ear as he enters her. It does not take very long until her climax. It's a stunningly beautiful moment as I feel her body tensing, then she will sometimes grasp my arm or press her head back against me and then tremble in a deep amazing way. She breathes and her mouth drops open as the slightest gasp is audible. It's like holding a hummingbird in your hand.

I continue to hold and nurture her but pretty much once she has climaxed she rolls over to the other side of the bed (she hates the wet spot) and I take her place, generally on all fours or prone on the bed - so the Master can finish his lust in me. Once he is finished I clean him and he slides in bed beside his wife and holds and kisses her. Usually I am dismissed for the evening - or to go clean up the house before checking on their needs - and then I'll bring them wine and cheese or hot towels. I am then dismissed to go home.

His wife is one of those women that once she orgasms, she's done. So I've never really had to clean her with my mouth - though I have used a moist towel on her a few times with her permission. Many times after an event or day, he will just use me in the slave quarters then join her in bed when he's been satisfied. But on those rare occasions I am permitted to serve their marriage bed, I am truly grateful.

Does your Master love you? In any way?

_____ ~ /_____

Thank you for that interesting and deep question.

My Master has a wife who is his heart's desire and his soul mate. That kind of love should always be exclusively between them - and it is. He's not "in love" with me, and never shall be - nor me him. But - there is a mutual bond we share as man to woman, Master to slave.

There are different ways of loving. I care for him deeply as a person. I don't think you have intimate experiences that take both body and soul and not create a bond. That's what I think I am with my Master – bonded. Our trust goes deeper than many married couples. How many vanilla wives will let their husbands tie them to a bed and whip them with a single tail whip until they are near the edge of passing out – and trust the man to know exactly where the edge is and when to stop?

We are tied together by shared bodies, jokes, pain and pleasure. I don't need love from him – I have everything I could desire.

I know you say you are not in love with your
Master, which I believe. But does it make you
jealous to see him & his wife engage in sexual
activities? Also, I know you are not allowed to
masturbate, would you be allowed to have a
boyfriend?

Thanks for these great questions - the second one is
definitely an insightful one.

No, I do not feel jealous when my Master and his
wife have sex or are sexual with each other. That is the way
it should be. They are married. In a way it makes me very
happy. They have both been open about the fact that he
needed more than a vanilla life and if she hadn't consented
to letting him own a slave - it's possible they could have
lost their marriage over his frustration at her refusal to be
involved in BDSM. So, he can experience dominance,
roughness, and ownership with me and that frees him to
give her the gentle, attentive love she requires.

A slave can really only be owned by one Master or
system at a time. The truth is - I would not be interested in
a boyfriend or lover who did not dominate and own me. So,
I would never be able to have a boyfriend while I was his
slave. If I met someone I loved, I would have to ask to be
released from his estate to pursue a relationship. But, I have
no time, no desire, and no need for that right now in my
life. I am very happy to be simply owned and used.

Since your Master is married and you're not in love with him, do holidays like Valentine's Day make you sad? I mean no one is going to bring you flowers or anything. Does it bother you to be so disconnected?

Thanks for your question. I think that is one of the big questions people have when you don't live with your owner or you serve a couple.

No, Valentine's Day doesn't make me sad, and no, it is unlikely anyone is going to bring me flowers. But, I don't really like flowers that much anyway - so that's okay. I am devoted to my Master and his wife and I am happy to see them experience romantic love for one another and be a part of that.

The great news for me is that because of the bad weather, I am going to serve them dinner at their home, and serve them sexually for the evening. My sister is staying with my parents and my nieces are at a slumber party so I am going to spend the night at my Master's house (probably in my slave quarters after I am dismissed) and I will get to make them breakfast and serve them breakfast in bed, as well as any morning service that might inspire. So not only am I excited about the day - I feel like I won the lottery.

Valentine's is about love. Being a slave owned by the Master is what I love. So - it's a perfect day. I hope you have the best holiday as well whether you are in a relationship, anticipating one, or enjoying time on your own.

I'm curious how Valentine's Friday was spent; would you mind relating to us the day's events?

———————————～———————————

Thank you for asking. I had a wonderful Friday night and Saturday morning serving my Master and his wife. It was a lot of work, and even more enjoyment. I got the opportunity to spend the night with my Master and his wife, and serve them in the morning as well. I am truly a blessed slave to have been able to do so.

I had a few surprises and it's good for me when things challenge and surprise me. The Lady asked their maid service the day before to get out the tablecloth and open the china hutch. Unfortunately, the maid set the cloth out in a lump and there were fingerprints all over the china - so a hurry-up ironing and cleaning had to be done that I wasn't counting on. While I was preparing dinner the Lady came home early so I could bathe and prepare her (hair, makeup, clothing) as well. I am very excited for my Master's wife that she is growing in her comfort zone regarding my slavery, but the two unexpected events really pushed my time schedule and stretched me. All did get done before the Master's arrival, thank goodness.

One of the best surprises was when my Master arrived home. The Lady decided she wanted me in a serving dress (a type of plain black dress I usually wear when accompanying them publicly) for dinner so I excused myself to change and the Master came with me into the slave quarters and gave me a very nice OTK and paddle spanking before I changed. That took all the stress away and it was wonderful to serve warm food with a very warm bottom.

For dinner I made arugula salad, stuffed mushrooms, crab Portofino over spaghetti and had picked up a chocolate mousse cake for dessert, served with a spicy

Italian wine. Everything went smoothly and they were satisfied and happy when I settled them with coffee as they watched a romantic movie and I cleaned up the kitchen, had my own dinner, and then knelt in service.

The Master decided it was time to continue the evening in bed, where I was allowed to undress the Lady, and then prepare them both orally for their intimacy, after which the Master used my body to complete his sexual experience to climax, and I climaxed as well - what a joy. He asked me to stay in bed with them for a while and we spent a lot of time kissing, holding and indulging in one another. That was new and nice. Eventually, the Master dismissed me and told me to wear a plug to bed as he wanted to use me in the morning.

I slept in the bed in the slave quarters (a spare bedroom set aside for me). Early the next morning the Master came in and without saying one word, grabbed my hips, positioned me face down/ass up on the bed and used me anally, somewhat roughly, then patted my rear as an affirmation and went back to bed. It was amazingly erotic to me to be taken and discarded so casually in silence, with nothing but my whimpers and gasps beneath him for sound.

I showered, made them a big breakfast which I served them in bed, kneeling beside the bed for their needs, and I was dismissed to go home. I was so sore/tired/happy I slept the rest of Saturday. I do not get to stay overnight very often and the whole thing was fantastic. Honestly, I have to say being used in the morning that way will always be a lovely memory.

Thanks for great report, kate. Did the Lady want you dressed plainly so there would be no distraction from her elegant self-presentation (whereas you, naked and collared, standing or kneeling, will always catch your Master's eye)? Are you open for more Domming from her? Is that a limit to be discussed with Him?

———————————~———————————

Thank you for this question and the positive affirmation. My Master's wife is indeed growing more comfortable and pleased with her husband's ownership of me and that makes us all very happy. However, I do want to clarify something.

My Master's wife is not a Dom and does not Dom me. She is very sweet and kind and has always been very generous and nice to me as well. I think it takes a very special woman to let her husband own and have sex with another without complaint or concern. I also think it works because they are not both "Doms" – I am owned by him. She is his wife and his passion – thus, when I serve her, I am serving him. She asks me to do things to make her more happy or comfortable – that's it. It wasn't a Dom kind of request at all. It went like this:

The Lady: I think the black dress for dinner service, don't you?

Master: Yes, I think that would look better. kate, wear the black dress.

Me: As you say, Sir. Please excuse me.

Chances are she decided to have me in a serving dress because it didn't fit the dinner or occasion to have me naked. She is an artist in her spare time so she has a good eye for what "looks right" and is aesthetically pleasing. For serving and preparing food I have a matching thong and waist apron I wear for hygienic purposes, along with my collar. But the dress added more class to the event.

My Master's wife has no reason to feel jealous or competition in any way. I am an owned sexual and personal servant of her husband, nothing more. One of the reasons we work well is that my Master truly loves his wife and nothing really takes the focus off of her. It is also my goal when I am serving them to be as invisible as possible so he can focus on her as well. Pleasing her pleases him – and that is what I am tasked to do and love to do. I enjoy pleasing her, because I do like her and as far as I can tell, she likes me too.

In terms of limits – when you are a slave there is no discussion. My limits were set when I gave my consent for his ownership and he placed his collar around my neck. There is no more discussion.

Does your Master ever give you a present? Like birthday or Christmas? Has he and his wife ever taken you to dinner just for you. If they did, would they make you serve them at the dinner?

Thank you for asking this fun question. Yes, my Master does give me birthday presents, Christmas presents, little things he saw in a store that reminded him of me, etc. That's part of any relationship - even Master/slave. They give lovely gifts that always seem perfect. Who knows me better than my own Master?

They have invited me to dinner as their guest, and I did serve them - because it's natural and a habit. If the Lady tried to pour coffee for me I think I would feel odd, because that's not my comfort zone.

I would like to change the frame on the thought, however. My Master and his wife do not "make" me serve them. Ever. They allow me to serve them and I am very grateful for the chance.

Has your Master ever whipped you in front of his wife? In front of others? Does that make it worse, better, or no effect? And lastly, has the Master's wife ever asked that you be punished?

─────────────── ～ ───────────────

Thank you for these great questions. My Master's wife is vanilla and is growing into loving her role as the wife of a slave owner (she does not like to be called Mistress, but "Lady"). She is not interested in whippings/spankings/ etc. My initial spanking to redden my rear in order to make my body appropriate to serve them is done in the "slave quarters" (a spare bedroom they use to keep all the BDSM fun stuff in, and where I am whipped and used). So she hears the punishment - but isn't a part of it. Discipline whippings or fun whippings (usually the latter, I don't require much correction) are done on Friday afternoons while she is at work.

The Master's wife does not nor has she ever asked for me to be punished nor does she really care much about that part.

I have been whipped at social gatherings (for fun, not correction) and it does heighten the arousal and suffering to listen to others laugh, comment or enjoy your pain. If I were to be whipped for an error in front of them, I would be mortified. Discipline is a serious affair between a Master and a slave, not a show.

When you join your Master's wife for a weekday lunch, do you have any special protocols? To an outsider it may simply look like a friendly meal between two professional women, but she is one of the few people who regularly sees your "true nature" openly displayed. Do you have subtle ways of conveying your servitude to her even at lunch? The way all three of you play in public is hot (at least to me) and I hope it is for all three of you!

―――――――――――――⌇―――――――――――――

Thank you for this fun question. We try to be true to the nature of our relationship, but at the same time we are not obvious about it when in public. I will do things like wait for her to order first, or if they leave a pitcher of water on the table I will fill her glass. One time she left her glasses in her car and couldn't read the menu so I went and got them. Small things that show my respect and service - but mostly we just chat about work, flowers, plans, etc. I always wait for her to stand to leave the table before I stand, etc.

Usually when she leaves she will give me a quick "business women's friend" hug and I will whisper in her ear "I am devoted to you" or "I adore you." If her husband was not my Master - and we had met at the ballet in a social community group, I think we would have been good friends anyway - she's quite lovely and kind.

Domestic Service

The Slave Speaks

Anyone who practices BDSM for more than a few months can tell you one emphatic truth: It's not just about sex. In fact, in lifestyle Dom/sub or Master/slave relationships, sex has very little to do with everyday life. Obedience, devotion, attitude and discipline are far more pervasive in a relationship based on power exchange. Domestic service is a delightful part of consensual slavery and I love it.

If, on the surface, domestic service doesn't seem like much – then you're doing it wrong. Domestic service isn't just doing the dishes or folding the clothes. It's not tossing together a dinner or washing the car. Those are chores. Domestic service is when you do those things with excellence, devotion and with your Master at the center of everything you do. Domestic service isn't just washing a glass. It is steaming that glass and polishing it until it sparkles for your Master's water. It is making sure his dinner has extras (including a garnished, attractive plate), and his tie is knotted perfectly. In short, it is making your Master feel like a million bucks, because he's worth even more than that to you.

Like most people, when it comes to my personal life I barely have time for the basics – getting my clothes in the washer and making sure I have enough clean dishes to get me through dinner. But, when it comes to my Master and the Lady – everything feels different, looks different and suddenly I have all the time in the world to take care of every detail and lavish them in my skill.

You don't have to spend a lot of money, do fancy things or take classes in gourmet cooking and stain removal. All you really need to do is invest in your

Master's service with style, grace and that little something extra that shows your devotion.

The truth is, anyone can give a blowjob and even the most amazing one eventually feels like every other one in the back of your Master's mind. But the way he feels when he sits down to a dinner you made, with a well set table, steamed glasses, polished silver, and you serving his every need will give him a memory and a feeling that is unique, beautiful and lasts forever.

I love your blog. My Master and I talk about your ideas all the time. Here's my question. I already know all the sex stuff. What else can I learn to please my Master and be a good slave? I want to be the ultimate slave.

⁓

Thank you, fellow servant, for the lovely compliment. Being the ultimate slave is a high goal indeed and I wish you every success.

Slavery isn't just sex - but it's good you have a full list of sexual willingness and abilities. I hope you will be open to more sexual knowledge though. I have found there are always new things to learn - and that's exciting.

Other things that are good to know -

1. How to serve coffee or tea without spilling it. How to make coffee and tea (from loose leaves - steeping and serving it right).

2. How to set a table correctly (silverware in place, etc.) and how to fold napkins decoratively - nothing makes a Master feel pampered than a well set table (particularly if he has guests over).

3. Everything about wine and champagne. How to serve it, what wine pairs with what food, how to open it, how to aerate red wine, what wines your Master enjoys.

4. Everything about cocktails. From fun shooters to traditional cocktails like Bourbon and Branch - learn recipes for drinks and how they are supposed be served. Also learn beer if he drinks that - learn how to get the right amount of head for the beer.

5. Tie a Tie. When I was married to my Master he never tied a tie for himself. Learn good looking knots and make him shine when he goes out.

6. Sew Buttons and seams - he has a favorite shirt that loses a button - fix it for him.

7. Massage - Don't just rub his back. Learn the techniques for proper massage so you are ready if he has a sore spot or just wants comfort (remember, avoid the spine). Learn how to handle hot towels and refreshing aftercare. If you're really good, learn to shave him.

8. Cooking – Find recipes he likes, fancy or not so fancy desserts, special treats only you can make for him. Learn presentation - make things taste good and look good.

9. Folding - The proper way to fold a shirt, sheets, hang pants, etc.

10. Learn what he is interested in and how you can support it. It doesn't matter whether he likes NASCAR, computer games, car shows or bird watching - how can you make his joy more enjoyable?

That's a small list - but I hope it helps you achieve your goal.

Do you go barefooted like a submissive woman
should?

Thank you for this interesting question. In service,
I usually am either barefoot or in high heels (and a collar
but nothing else). It depends on what I'm doing. If I'm
there to be disciplined, serve in regular ways or simply
please him - I am barefoot. If I am there for his visual and
sexual pleasure, at a fancy event or to promote his status, I
am usually in black stilettos.

I grew up in the country where going barefoot was a
way of life so I enjoy it. I also enjoy the power and lift a
girl gets from a nice set of heels. Whatever pleases my
Master I'm happy to accept.

You make formal dinners for your Master and Mistress. How do you do that since you don't live there? Do you cook it at your house and take it over? Do you sit at the table and eat with them? If not, when do you eat? What about clean up? I want to make a nice dinner for this Master who did training with my Master and me at His house for him and his sub but I'm not sure what to do.

Hello Sister Servant,

Thank you for these lovely questions. I think offering to make a meal for your training Master and his sub is a beautiful idea. My first suggestion would be to ask your Master to make the offer to the other Master, and take it from there.

Usually when my Master and the Lady want a formal dinner it is to celebrate something at her job or his or a small joy of some kind. The Master will arrange the date with me (usually a Friday since I have a half-day off - but not always) in advance and tell me what they would like. Salmon, tenderloin, Italian crusted chicken - whatever. If there is a new recipe his wife finds he will usually email it to me in advance (that way I can make a batch at home and test it out first).

On the day of the dinner I stop by the bakery on the way in and get a pastry of some kind for dessert (I cook well, but pastry defies me. It takes a genius to make good pastry). Then on the way to their house I stop by the store and get what I need for dinner.

If we are celebrating something for her - I also get some edible orchids or white chocolate for a garnish. If it's for him - I get Jameson to leave a shot by his plate. I almost always pick up some fresh flowers for the table.

I have a key and alarm codes to their house -so I let myself in, go to the slave quarters and change into the half apron/thong combo I wear while cooking, put my collar on, and cook the meal/set the table. If they come home while dinner is in progress I'll offer them a drink and get them settled.

I never eat with them when serving dinner. I usually pack a dinner (like packing lunch) and eat while I'm preparing their dinner. Generally I stand in the back of the room and wait in case they need/want something while dinner is served. Normally, I try to be invisible so they can enjoy their dinner. When dessert is over I get them settled in the den with coffee or a drink and clean the kitchen. When it is all finished I kneel before the Master to see if he requires or desires service (he generally enjoys oral service after dinner), or sometimes he just dismisses me. I get dressed and go. It's a lot of fun, but only happens maybe once every 3 or 4 months. I'd do it more if I had time. I love it.

I hope you get to enjoy the gift of giving to your Master's friend.

Is there a reason you don't eat any of the beautiful foods you prepare for your Master and bring your own "packed dinner" to eat as you prepare their feast?

———————～——⁄———————

Thank you so much for this lovely note and compliment. I appreciate your words greatly.

To answer your question, I don't eat the food I make for their celebrations for a couple of reasons, some practical and some attitudinal.

1. I don't have time. My goal is to have the food hot and ready when the Master and the Lady arrive home from work or close to time. In order to do that I have to get cooking, table setting, glass polishing (hot water steam and cloth), silverware polished, and everything done by the time they sit down. Once they are eating I need to be in position in the room for their needs, and afterward I try to clean quickly so as to serve them in their den. The Master's wife is a fast eater and he eats more slowly so I need to cater to her needs while he finishes. So I don't have time to sit down and eat. Bites of a sandwich, veggies, grapes or something I can pop in my mouth as I work are better for me.

2. It's easier to cook for two than three. There is symmetry and ease in making dinner for two and most of my recipes are for two (since they are romantic dinners usually) – adding a third salmon steak or chicken breast just adds to the effort/time.

3. It is not my dinner, but theirs. A slave may eat from (if not at) the Master's table only by invitation and I do not generally have that invitation. There are times when the Master will say (particularly about a pastry I've picked up) "kate, try one of these, or kate, have some of this

braised asparagus – you did well" and I will thank him and try it in the kitchen.

Serving is such a great rush and feeling I am always fed more by their satisfaction than the food would do anyway.

My Mistress requires I wear lace thong panties at all times while I'm not with her. I find them uncomfortable and prefer cotton during the day. Would you disobey your Master when not with him - like at work, or doing chores? Mistress says service to her is 24/7/365 whenever, wherever. What should I do?

———————————— ～ ————————————

Thank you so much for writing me. We are always stronger servers together. First and foremost – all praise, respect and honor to your Mistress. It is always a slave's duty to honor someone in such authority as she – and I do honor her and hope nothing I say offends.

I do not disobey my Master, but he also does not provoke my disobedience. His view is the same as your Mistress and it is my view as well – he owns me 24/7/365. But, he also understands that with ownership comes responsibility. He does not suggest I do anything that interferes with my job. No butt plugs at work, special panties, or phone calls at certain times, etc. His only commands for me at work are that I use respect with all people, act with proper demeanor, do excellent work and fulfill my duties to my employer.

He knows that my profession and the career I have worked to achieve is of value to him, and he also understands my salary supports myself plus 5 other people so he will not jeopardize what is important. I would have no need to disobey him at work because he doesn't push that boundary. And, there are plenty of other places he can make me wear a plug.

If your Mistress offers you a chance to ask for permission to speak freely, you might want to tell her that the lace thong is a command you can't obey or is too much – and offer the reasons why. How she reacts is her right and choice. But, I feel it is better to be honest with her than disobey her. Even if your honest situation disappoints her – at least she will know she can trust you. And trust is worth the world.

There is a sister servant online whom I like and respect – she told me not long ago that she once ended up telling her Master about something she didn't think she could do. He strapped her for the conversation/denial but also honored her request. That is the essence of a great servant – even when she knew it might bring her punishment – she still told the truth and it changed the situation.

My best to you and your Mistress. The fact you are distressed about this shows your devotion to her, and I hope she will see that as well.

My Master and I talk about moving in together one day and starting a family. I work full- time, his work is less stringent and allows for more flexibility. We would like to engage in some variation of TPE at home. Yet, we're both struggling with how domestic duties factor in such a relationship that's still rife with expectations on my part.

Thank you so much for asking me. Planning for a future is always an exciting time - and hooray (!) for planning. The best TPE relationships have a healthy balance of design in them.

The great news for all of us is that there is no rigid, "do this, not that" in BDSM. You can be a sub with some slave habits, a slave with some sub requirements, or a combo: slave but every once in a while little girl - and as long as it works for you two - it's all good.

The thing that challenges most real life TPE relationships is lack of flexibility. Your Master's protocol for you needs to be able to bend and move as situations change. A musician must tune a guitar and then re-tune it through a series of songs. Your relationship will also need re-tooled from time to time as jobs, kids, energy levels, etc. come into play.

The Master is the head of the relationship, but he also has responsibilities to the relationship. There is nothing that suggests you have to do every chore because you're a sub. Decide what duties he wishes you to perform, and make sure you perform them with excellence. That's really all a wise Master expects - is your excellence in what you do. Not that you do every single thing ever. If he is at home and there are dishes, he can do them. If he says dishes are your job, then do them well. It doesn't make him less of a Master to do the dishes. It makes him a stronger Master because he too cares for the household.

If something is not working - you have too many chores, or too little time for sexy fun or whatever - ask for his permission to sit down and re-plan. Budget your energy/time like you would budget money. You are a valuable asset just like finance. Together you two can figure out the best uses.

OMG kate! I read your post a long time ago about serving tea and I thought that would be perfect for my Master for Valentine's - to serve tea and dessert for him. So I went and bought nice tea and this teapot and I have been practicing and the tea goes everywhere. If I don't hold the lid the tea comes out and if I do hold the lid it just drips all over the table. HELP!

———

Thanks for reading my post and giving such an elegant gift to your Master. Don't worry - you'll get this down.

1. You need to stay a little calmer. Pouring tea well is an art form (but once you learn the feel of it - it's a breeze). Remember, confidence is always more sexy than chaos. So - take some deep breaths. Calm and center. It's gonna be fine.

2. The trick is - you're trying too hard. Teapots are designed to pour tea. That means you don't have to pour it. You just have to give it the right angle and get out of its way. You are likely inverting the teapot too much so that it is pouring more than it can accommodate at one time.

3. You DO need to hold the lid on most tea pots. That's your job. Here's a step by step.

- After the tea has steeped the right amount of time take the strainer or bags out.
- Place the teacup on a flat surface where you can pour into it (do not hold it).
- Hold the handle of the teapot in your most used hand (right handed, right hand, etc.), and hold the lid down with the other.
- Slightly angle the pot down until the tea starts to dribble then pour smoothly. DO

NOT HURRY. Tea is not about speed (and, I am usually naked when pouring tea or coffee for the Master so I don't like boiling splashes). Let the tea slowly come out of the spout into the cup. If you try to go too fast, you will tip the pot too far and it will pour/drip all over.

- Only when the tea begins to slow down should you angle it any more downward. Let the teapot do to the work. Just give it enough of an incline for the tea to pour.
- When you see the cup is near 3/4 full slowly pull back (don't jerk) until the tea stops. Set your pot down.

And Ta-da! - Tea and elegance for the Master.

And remember: If you lose your grip and pour tea all over the table the world won't end. You are trying to do an act of devotion. A wise Master will know that, and love you for it - no matter what happens.

Good luck and have a wonderful evening,

I'm the one who asked you about tea for my Master for Valentine's. I wanted to thank you because it worked out sooo perfectly. I didn't spill AND made cookies to go with it. He was so happy. Then last week I made him a big dinner and served it to him and – wow - he was excited and we made love like crazy after that. He said being served like that is better than all the "Sirs" in the world. I want to keep doing it but we don't have much money for fancy stuff. Any ideas?

Thank you so much for letting me know how it went. I was wondering and hoped it went alright for you. Now I see you've helped your Master learn a great secret - the relationship, the serving, and the effort is what makes things rich, deep and lovely. Consensual slavery and submission is not just about sex and Sirs. You've tapped into the vein of gold in this life.

You don't have to spend a lot of money to make a fancy dinner. What matters is the way you present the food, and the love you make it with. What he's enjoying isn't just the food - he's tasting your devotion and no money in the world can buy that.

Boneless chicken is pretty inexpensive and you can do almost anything with it. Bake it, shred it, put in on a bed of rice with some broccoli/cheese soup and it's a delicious casserole. Salads with different lettuces or a little bit of rolled turkey lunch meat, some flavored cheese spread and an olive with pimento on a toothpick looks fun. One of my Master's favorite things for me to make is cheese enchiladas that cost about 8 dollars to make. But, served on a glass plate with a glass of sangria by the hand

of a woman who dedicated her life and body to his pleasure
- it's a feast.

Enjoy!

I appreciate that you prefer to be "dismissed" after service, not held and cuddled. Does your Master have a range of phrases to dismiss you, from very curt ("dismissed") to what a more formal style of dismissing a servant, "Thank you, kate" (perhaps after an evening of gracious service). Do you respond differently to various forms of dismissal?

———————————⌇———————————

Thank you for asking this question. It gives me a chance to lean back and think about his tone of voice and the pleasure I get at night knowing he has been satisfied.

My Master uses a few different phrases but there doesn't seem to be any real difference in tone or meaning - just different circumstances. He has never dismissed me angrily or unhappily - and I am thankful for that.

Usually if he's happy and about to go to sleep with his wife he will say, "that's all" or "you're dismissed" in a half yawn or with a slight hand wave. Sometimes if it's been a more special dinner or evening he will say, "That was lovely, kate" or "Well done," as he nods and waves toward the door. To clarify - I always say, "Thank you, Sir. I will go now." And sometimes he will give me a task or chore on my way out such as, "Make sure the dishes are in the cupboard" or "Please grab my shirts for the dry cleaners on the way out." To which I thank him and go.

He compliments me frequently and if there was something he wanted differently, he would tell me. So I generally thank him no matter what the send off, put my clothes on, set their alarm and go on my way so they can rest and enjoy the night.

The Lady is very soft spoken and kind. She will generally say, "Thank you, kate" and more than once has kissed me on the cheek before I am dismissed. It's a lovely gesture and I am thankful for her graciousness.

Angry Anons

The Slave Speaks

The majority of questions I get online are from anonymous askers (Anons). I like the ability to ask anonymously because it usually creates an environment where people can ask questions without shame and get the real answers they need. However, every yin has a yang and the flip side of anonymous questions that offer help are anonymous questions and comments designed to hurt. For some reason, I get my share of angry Anons.

I answer all of my Anons respectfully, except for messages that threaten me, are violently sexually graphic, or just contain long strings of profanity. I feel that someone who gets a thrill over being rude or pushy should not be allowed to go unchallenged. I also realize in a subculture where treating a woman like an object is sometimes what she wants – it's hard for folks to realize they are being inappropriate. So, I answer them with as much respect and gentility as my defense can muster.

I'm not very surprised when I get an email full of misogyny from a misogynist, or when I get a nasty note from an angry vanilla woman who feels BDSM is threatening her right to missionary position sex every Saturday night from 9:15 to 9:20. What I am surprised about is the number of women willing to attack or boss around other women. Slave or free, sub or vanilla – we should stand together. Yet, I've sustained a number of attacks by self-proclaimed feminists (who never seem to understand they are supposedly feminists because they don't want society telling a woman who to be, but they are telling me who not to be) and female subs/slaves who feel I'm not edgy, strong, young or bratty enough.

Perhaps the most intriguing queries were a series of increasingly accusing and hateful emails about the Amish. That was odd since I'm not Amish. But, because I also grew up in a religion without a television, somehow I was guilty by association. The rest of the ugly came from more familiar sources – people who hate BDSM, misogynists who worry I'm not being called a slut enough, and one man who was horrified beyond belief that road head (having oral sex while driving) is on my limit list.

Angry anons make me do two things.

First – they make me laugh. We all have such a small amount of time in a day to enjoy, work and play. Who wants to spend their time writing angry notes to strangers? I'm always left thinking, "Wow, due to the miracle of the internet you can ask me any question in the world and you've chosen to harp on my age and whether or not my breasts hang low. Really?"

Second – they fill me with pity. How tragic must someone's life be that the only way they feel good is to write ugly anonymous notes on the internet? I always pity their lack of manners. (Can a misogynist walk up to any woman in a real bar and say, "Hey slut, you're nothing but a set of holes" and get by with it? I think not. They must be very lonely.). I am always sorry to see their flawed logic, desperate assertions and horrid spelling and grammar. I want to reach out to them, hug them and say, "Stop complaining for a minute, baby. It'll be okay."

Through the sad, outrageous and all-too-common messages of the angry Anons, I think we all have some things to learn:

1. *It takes an equal amount of energy to politely correct them as to type cuss words at them, and you feel better in the long run by putting more good words in the world than bad.*
2. *Life is too short to get caught up in the drama. Laugh it off and move forward.*

3. *They aren't really writing about you. They don't know you.*

4. *Just because you're a consensual slave or a submissive doesn't mean you can't defend yourself. As my training Master used to say, "You can put any part of your body you choose in a slave's mouth, but never forget – she still has teeth."*

You should be an Alpha Sub like me. You are educated, strong and experienced but you just lay down and take whatever your Master says. Alpha Subs are defiant and sassy. I don't just bend over when he says. I make him engage my mind. I push his assumptions. I don't follow at a snap. I say, "No." I ask why. If the Dom is smart enough for me he will challenge my brain and then he gets my body. Not to insult you but your way seems a little weak. Try Alpha Subbing.

Thank you for this brash comment, Anon. I am so relieved you were not trying to insult me.

I am happy that you have found a philosophy and way of being that suits your nature. However, what is apparent in your comment is a lot of "I" and absolutely no "we." I'm not interested in having the focal point of my sexuality be a narcissistic serving of my needs. I am interested in having my sexuality meet the needs of my Master and of our relationship - Master to slave.

I don't need to judge your flashy oxymoron label - but I can say that it simply isn't necessary for me to be labeled by anyone but my Master, who calls me his property.

I am strong enough to take my mind, my time, my body and kneel naked before the Master enduring all he will use, take, whip and kiss. That's strong enough for me. If it is not strong enough for you - that is unfortunate. And irrelevant.

Why don't you cuss like everyone else? Do you think you're better than us? I'm not ashamed to say I'm a fuckpig. You make the word "cock" sound like a damn flower arrangement.

    Thanks for this interesting question and statement. I'm sure it wasn't your intent - but it did make me smile this morning.

    Every person has their own way. You should never be ashamed to be a fuckpig. It seems to offer you a lot of pleasure. People are not better than each other. We are all just different.

    I don't cuss for a number of reasons, I suppose:

1. I was raised in a family where that was not permitted and brought quite a severe punishment. So, cussing isn't my default.
2. There are usually more descriptive words to use.
3. I spent a good amount of time training and living as an Odalisque and foul language is not a part of that life. The view is that a slave's words should be as soft and pleasing as her body.
4. My current slavery and slave mindset includes a lot of the Odalisque philosophy only there is more whipping and chores involved - so cussing still just isn't part of the plan.

    Please don't be distressed. If my Master wants me to talk dirty in his ear while he takes me I can rattle off a string of sexual profanity so vile that it will singe the pubic hair right off his body.

As for flower arrangements, well — there are a lot of edible flowers in the world.

How can you even dare to call yourself a woman?
You advocate everything that oppresses women
and they fight against. I'm a feminist. You're just a
cocksucking sellout.

——————————～———/——————————

Thank you for this angry little note. While I assume
these questions and thoughts are just part of a rhetorical
outburst designed to make you feel better - I would like to
be polite enough to answer. After all, you are a guest in my
inbox.

So - I can call myself a woman because I am one.
Gender is a complex combination of genitalia, hormone
balances, and brain identification patterns. So - since I have
a vagina and am full of estrogen, along with the gender
identification pattern of a female - I can call myself a
woman.

These things I say and think don't oppress women
who choose this life by their own will and enjoy it.
Actually - what oppresses women are self-proclaimed
feminists who think there is only one way to be a woman -
your way.

You're correct - I do suck cock. A lot. And I love it.

You're incorrect - I'm not selling anything. I give it
all away for free.

I hope life brings you whatever balance or power
you are lacking that leads you to strike out at strangers
without a leg to stand on. You will be in my best thoughts.

Honestly, your parents ought to be kissing your ass because you take care of them after they gave their property to a male relative, bypassing their daughters, the rightful heirs. And you're smart to have chosen an education and a decent job to provide for them. Where you got your compassion for them is anyone's guess.

———————————～———————————

Thanks for your thoughts. I think your thinking mirrors what many think about that issue and I love the passion in your writing. This is just a question of culture.

I got my sense of compassion from my parents, who love me and my sisters a great deal. We grew up in a very strict home, but it was full of security, love, laughter - and a lot of garden vegetables. :)

In the culture of my parents and their community, women are not rightful heirs to anything. In their community girls go all the way through high school then have a choice - care for their parents/home or get married. If a girl chooses college or single life - they leave the community/faith, which all three of my parent's daughters did - so I think they have some disappointments of their own.

They allowed us to go, and encouraged us in our studies and lives. If we had stayed in the community - one of our husbands would have gotten our family farm - but we didn't so it went to a male cousin who did not have land of his own (he is a 3rd born son). My parents didn't do anything to hurt me - they did what their culture says to do.

Every culture has its own ideas of right and wrong - and it is better to learn and appreciate than to judge. The ability to accept a different path empowered me to embrace my sexual slavery, my intense and constant desires to be used, and accept others as they are - even my parents.

You <u>do</u> realize that feminism is the reason you can do what you do, right? Feminism means you get to choose your lifestyle, as opposed to having it chosen for you because of your gender. Don't blame us for judgment. You can't say we didn't give you the freedom.

———————

1. I think you over-estimate feminism and what it's done.

2. I think you over-estimate your right or ability to tell me what I can and cannot say or who I can and cannot blame.

3. I think you highly underestimate western culture if you really think feminism, or history, was ever changed by someone named anonymous.

Whoa, slave kate, you're a spunky girl. You're our favorite slave! Love how you deny feminism even as it benefits your life, like your administrative job, which allows you to support your folks and your slave lifestyle. If it wasn't for feminism, you'd be homeless after your ex-Master dumped you. Keep your chin down and carry on!

———————————————

Oh ladies, you're so young - it's precious. Please let me clear some things up for you - as I know opinionated young women like yourselves do so enjoy being right.

1. I am a Senior Executive and Department Chair of Research. I'm not an administrator.

2. I know this will shock you but women went to college <u>before</u> feminism. They've been graduating with medical degrees and all kinds of amazing things since the late 1850's (beating feminism by over 100 years). So, no - feminism did not allow me to go to college.

3. I got my Bachelors and Masters degrees through school-founded scholarships (not gender based ones), and my Ph.D. fellowship was paid for by a governmental grant for research. Again - feminism didn't pay for my college.

4. Feminism has played an important role in showcasing women's rights. However - it hasn't gotten an equal pay for women bill passed in congress, created equal opportunities in my workplace, or paid my mortgage - although you appear to believe I was found in a trash can living off of discarded chicken bones until a feminist rescued me and put me in a glass house.

5. When you're a grown up - it's not called "dumped." It's called divorced - and in my case it was a mutual and beneficial decision.

So – no, I'm not here because of feminism. In fact, <u>many</u> women existed and did amazing things before modern feminism burned its first bra. I do stand on the shoulders of many women who voiced and fought for everything from the right to vote, to an understanding of women's health care needs. I am thankful and respectful to them — which is far more than you have been to me.

Do you know of any other Amish women who identify as sexually submissive? I know it's a patriarchal religion, but do you think it translates into being a female sub from childhood? Also, do you know of any Dommes that grew up Amish? My guess would be if they're Dommes, they're not Mennonite or Amish any more.

———————————————————————

Thank you for these questions. Please understand - I am not Amish. I was raised in a Mennonite community which is similar in some ways but very different in others. Pretty much any woman asserting herself sexually (either learning about sex enough to ask to be a sub, or being a Domme) has left the Mennonites behind. Girls are kept very innocent of all things sexual. Getting caught kissing before marriage will earn you severe punishment. So, a woman who marries and stays in the faith won't know about "sexual submission" because there is only one way to have sex - her husband's way. When the whole world is made of submissive women - it's not something you have to identify as. It's just a fact.

When I got married my mother insisted on giving me the traditional "sex talk" the night before. She knew I was not a virgin, but said it was a tradition she looked forward to. So - I listened. And - it had <u>nothing</u> to do with how to have sex. It was about how a woman honors a man by being soft beneath him, and he enters her as a sign of following God's command to be fruitful, but there must be pain of plowing the field before the fruit can be planted. Then she told me every man has his own rhythm, and no matter what my body wants, my job is to follow his rhythm. That's the whole sex talk.

For ex-Mennonites, I'm sure many are attracted to "taken in hand" or "50's style" marriages - where male dominance and spanking are still in force. The world is very chaotic when you leave the community. It is loud, distracted with entertainment, and there are no clear decisions or consequences. So, many ex-Mennonite women seek out a man who will provide the security of structure and give them order to submit to. Most of the women I know who left have dominant or at least controlling husbands, and strong family roles.

It is a different world. There are many orders of Mennonites and Amish - but they tend to agree; a man's place is at the head of his table and the wife's place is to honor him and submit to him in all things.

Your reply to the Amish/Menn. women question got me thinking. What about Amish men? Are they raised to be dominant? Who teaches them about sex? Do you know of any Amish Doms? Or do they live the domestic discipline lifestyle? Just curious here--you never hear anything about Amish sex!

———————⟋～⟍———————

Thank you for your question. You never hear about Amish sex because they probably don't talk about it with each other, let alone some outsider. Again, I am not Amish and can't truly speak to their experience.

I think you are having trouble understanding the Mennonite community because you are trying to understand them as part of your world. Mennonites live in an entirely different world than you. There are no Doms, DD, Daddies, vanilla or anything with sex as an identifier. They aren't raised to be dominant. They are raised to be men.

There are only 2 roles in the whole Mennonite world:

Man

Woman

That's it. The man is in charge. He makes all decisions, owns all property, handles all money, reads and teaches the Bible, disciplines the children (physical discipline for children, not wives. By the time you are a wife you wouldn't need physical discipline. If you disobey as a wife you are taken before the minister or your family is shunned or shamed.). Mennonites believe a man's family is a reflection on him. To disobey your husband is to bring shame on him, your children, and your parents. It isn't done.

Women: take care of the house, work in the field, take care of the children, sew the clothes, tend the needs, obey the man, remind the children of the rules and tells the father when they need discipline. Women nurture, obey, serve and love.

No one teaches men about sex. You aren't allowed to kiss or hold hands until you are married. There is no sex education (because of the strict lifestyle, there are also no STD's). Once married, men and women figure sex out by themselves - just like a lot of people.

I have a gal pal who dated an Amish boy during his rumspringa. She said he was the absolute worst at sex because he said oral sex was what animals did and he only had sex with her missionary style (w/lots of guilt too). What's your opinion of Amish men and sex? Are they really that ignorant or misguided about women's bodies?

————————————～———————————

Thank you for this entertaining story and questions. To answer you:

1. Mennonites are not the same as Amish. We don't have rumspringa, you stay or you go, we have electricity in our houses and drive cars - but no media, TV, etc. I was raised Old Order Mennonite. I am not Amish.

2. I've never had sex with an Amish man. It sounds dreadful.

3. I don't think of the Amish or Mennonites as "ignorant" - that seems harsh. What we are is "sheltered." It is true - we don't know anything about sex and aren't taught anything. When animals do it we are told that's nature and to not watch. But, we all watch because it is the only sex we ever see. Remember in our world there is:

- No TV
- No Radio (except weather reports)
- No Movies
- Only books our parents/church approve
- No outsiders
- No sex education

Where would we learn about sex from? Our parents tell us, "That is for married women/men." They give you a brief talk on your wedding night.

So, yep, if we leave the community - we go into the world knowing nothing. I got totally taken advantage of from my first boyfriend in college who told me that I had to suck his penis or he wouldn't be able to have sex because that's how a man got erect. I did it every time for almost 2 months until I mentioned to my older sister that it was taking a long time for his penis to be ready and she nearly fell down laughing and explained reality to me.

But there is a lot of love, strength, loyalty and goodness in communities like the Mennonite or Amish. They are good people who make beautiful children, and have lifelong love. Just not the way we do.

When did you realize you had a good mind that wanted to learn and be challenged? I just saw the PBS special on the Amish and, although I know you were not Amish, I did get depressed (appropriately!) when I saw how little educational opportunity is available in such closed, conservative communities, especially for girls.

Thanks so much for this question. I appreciate your concern for others - particularly girls - but it's such a multi-layered equation.

Every culture on the outside has oddities - things we don't understand or like. In terms of Amish and Mennonite culture - they probably get depressed for us. My mother once told me, "I cried when each of you moved out, because the world is so terrible." They think women are "forced" into careers because families need two working parents because there is so much expectation to buy things. Think about it - my parents raised a family of three girls on what was probably a $20,000 a year salary in today's money, at best. They think women have to do all the work (work out of the home, work in the home, have the children, care for the children), and it is tragic the way people speak to us and around us.

Farm life doesn't mean you're stupid. There are plenty of chances to learn things, use your mind, and figure stuff out living on a farm - I know people with a Ph.D. who can't keep a house plant alive, and my mother can grow a garden that feeds 5 people without using insecticide. I know some farmers who have rigged things in their barns that would rival a German car engineer. It's not learning or thinking Amish/Mennonite girls lack – it is just a difference in content.

Being Mennonite or Amish isn't better or worse than being in the modern world. It's just different.

There is a multitude of cases that point to rampant sexual abuse, especially of minors, in the Amish community. Having grown up in an area with noticeable populations of both Amish and Mennonite (I used to cut wood with a few Mennonites) I fully understand basic differences in the cultures. Without accusing you of glorifying the Amish culture, could you speak a little on any similar experiences you may have witnessed in your upbringing that are not just distasteful, but perhaps illegal?

———————————— ∽ ————————————

Thanks for your question. I have no reason to "glorify Amish culture." I am not Amish. I was not raised Amish. I have nothing to do with the Amish. Anon, I am beginning to believe your tone and numerous leading questions about the Amish community shows that you have unresolved personal issues that would be better pursued in a therapist's office and not a BDSM blog.

As for your question directly - I have never seen anything distasteful or illegal in the community I was raised. I did not see or experience anything sexual at all - let alone sexually inappropriate.

As a person who works in research I can tell you the words you choose: "multitude of cases" and "rampant" are completely leading and meaningless in real life research, evidence or even anecdotal understanding. If my intern sent that sentence to me, he or she would be at best reprimanded and more likely replaced. The Amish are a statistic minority, made up of a diverse number of small sects and communities - with different rules and ritual. To take a statistic sample that would lead to a conclusion like yours would require a culturally competent, multi-phasic study, peer reviewed and analyzed.

That said, here's the truth: As much as I hate this fact - sexual abuse exists.

- It exists in the Amish and Mennonite Community.
- It exists in the white, liberal educated community.
- It exists in the religious community (Catholics, Protestant, Buddhist, Muslim, Jewish communities).
- It exist in atheist and agnostic communities.
- It exist in every racial, social, economic, geographic and age community in the world.
- It exists.

And it's wrong. Always. Research and programs for the prevention, identification, and intervention for perpetrators and protection, therapeutic intervention and support for survivors need to be a priority for every community, not just the secluded religious communities.

I read on your blog you are in a religion that didn't watch TV or do normal stuff. But, you are super kinky. So it clearly didn't keep you pure or anything. Seems like your religion is wasting its time.

———————————⟋—————————

Thank you for this interesting note. I'm not sure if you are trying to ask me a question or are just making a statement. While it is rarely the job of a slave to correct a free person, there are several things unfortunately not factual or correct in your comment. Please allow me some explanation.

1. I am not in the faith of my parents. My parents are Old Order Mennonites and were farmers. I left their faith when I went to college.

2. Mennonites (as I was raised) do plenty of "normal stuff" - they eat, work, play, laugh, love, study, and build community bonds. They have very rigid roles for men and women, and avoid things that interrupt their peace/natural order. But - they are people like everyone else.

3. The point of avoiding TV and media is not to keep people "pure." Mennonites avoid TV and media because it interrupts the flow of daily life and brings unnatural (to them) elements into their day. If the TV is playing people don't talk to one another. TV shows things Mennonites don't want in their world- violence, alternate gender/family roles and commercialism.

4. The faith practiced by my parents is not a religion. If it is not something you live in daily practice I think all religion without living it is a waste of time. For my parents, Mennonite ideas are how they lived every day. The stuff you actually build your life out of is rarely a waste of time.

Hopefully that clears up any question you may have
had.

The aphorism "Power corrupts; absolute power corrupts absolutely" has been overwhelmingly true both politically and economically throughout history. During most of human history power has corrupted personal affairs also, from women and children being abused by husbands and fathers to outright slavery and dehumanizing cruelty. Doesn't power corrupt in erotic relationships?

───────────────

Thank you for this great question. What a wonderful thing to ponder.

BDSM relationships are often built on the "exchange" of power, not the accumulation of power. In consensual slavery, the Master has the power given by the slave. The slave has the power of consent that serves as a check and balance. A Master can abuse a slave, and in consensual slavery - the slave can say, "We are done here" and walk out.

Is there corruption in BDSM relationships? Yes. Does it come from the exchange of power? Not as much as it does the primary component: Human Beings.

The basic premise of a BDSM relationship is that both participants are:

- Adults
- Responsible for themselves
- Willing to engage
- Mentally, physically, and spiritually able to accommodate the relationship in a healthy way.

When those things are not present - the human flaws we carry create abuse and corruption.

For example: A woman is desperate for a father figure, she was abandoned as a child, she gets with a Master who treats her badly, but she cannot leave him because of her crippling abandonment issues and inability to stand up to him.

Is power the problem in that situation? No: The problems are:

1. The Master is abusive: (no matter what problems other people have, abusers are always responsible for abuse.). He is misusing his power. Power didn't make him an abuser, he probably came that way.

2. The woman doesn't need to be a slave/sub at this time. She needs interventional therapy. She needs to become more able to control her own environment and act not react. She is not ready for this arena.

Note: I have heard people say, "If I waited for all my issues to be solved in order to be a slave I would never become one." And my response is - "Then don't wait on them. Work on them." Seek help. Seek healing. Find situations that you can participate in with responsibility and safety.

In real life BDSM relationships control, power, and pain are the elements. This isn't a playground. This is major league trust. If you aren't equipped, in control, and able - don't step into this arena without a lot of work, guides, and help.

Safe Guards:

- Self-responsibility and awareness: Make sure you know what you are getting into and if you have concerns, issues or challenges - take steps to heal or manage them.

- Honesty: If you have a concern or challenge be honest with a play partner up front about your limits and needs.

- Act responsibly and wisely: If you can't be restrained because you are claustrophobic don't hook up with a guy named "Rope Master" who is a bondage fan and then complain when he wants to tie you up. Learn to say "No" and "Not You." Be willing to protect yourself and make wise choices about who you give power to.

- Act responsibly with power. Don't abuse. Don't manipulate. Don't be a predator who looks for the young, weak, mentally unhealthy girls to "dominate" - there's no glory in it (a bird with a broken wing is hardly a great catch), and it leads down a bad road for you both.

- Invest in community. We need to work together, talk to one another honestly, protect one another, and eradicate abusers from our community.

To follow up on my power question - the prison experiments conducted by Philip Zimbardo suggest that power has distorting effects on responsibility after controlling for social variables. There is a Wikipedia entry.

———————————～———————————

Thanks for that thought. The Stanford Prison Experiment, and Phillip Zimbardo's ethical misdeeds during the experiment have been the subject of mental health debate and public health history since the experiment occurred in 1971.

An aside: A "community written" encyclopedia without academic peer review should not be the only source of information and is not necessarily validated on its own merit. Most college professors today will tell you the same thing.

Let's look at BDSM, and then Zimbardo's behavior:

The basis of Zimbardo's conclusion makes good common sense and has been proven true time after time, including Abu Girab. It is simply this:

"Good people, when placed in adverse situations will act barbarically to cope or survive"

That is hardly the description of a healthy BDSM relationship. A Dom or a Master is rarely put in "adverse conditions" - this is about fun, sexual kink, identity and role orientation. None of those are specifically adverse - particularly for the power holder/Dom. The Master isn't coping or desperate to survive or please an outside source. He's taking a role in a mutually agreed upon relationship.

So the comparison between BDSM and the Stanford Prison Experiment is neither aligned nor effective. In short, apples and oranges.

In fact, while the experiment in no way resembles a real life BDSM relationship, you might be able to compare it to the fantasy misogynist porn online. Because both situations are about as real.

Zimbardo has come under a great deal of scrutiny because his research methods were both sloppy and manipulative. Zimbardo's interns pressured both guards and prisoners to "create results" and set up many of the situations themselves. Many "guards" said it was Zimbardo himself who suggested they use sleep deprivation to get the prisoners to react.

Case in point: Dave Eshelman, one of the more sadistic guards, says he was a drama student who was acting, and encouraged to act the part. He was told in the beginning by Zimbardo's people to "force the issues" and so he did. (Wall Street Journal, July 2011, "The Stanford Prison Experiment 40 Years Later" by Christopher Shea). In the same article a participant named John Mark who was a prisoner claimed to be stoned through the whole event and said Zimbardo wanted to bring it to a crescendo and pressured the situations to get worse.

Craig Haney, one of the research assistants, said they were worried that nothing would happen, that it would be boring or produce no results so they began to monkey with the design and make suggestions to create a more active experiment (Stanford Alumni Journal, August 2011, "The Menace Within" by Romesh Ratnesar).

So - while it has been a case study in psychology for years (mostly reviewed for the ethics of the study - not the conclusions) and it has been shown in many studies that participants in adverse conditions such as war, famine, oppression do react in barbaric ways —- Zimbardo's study does contain a great deal of manipulated scenarios to create its conclusions.

No one stands in a relationship between a Dom and sub and screams "I ORDER YOU TO GO IN THERE

AND BEAT HER UNTIL SHE BREAKS" - a BDMS relationship is not "oppression" - it is a consensual choice. A woman who puts on a collar willingly is not involved in war, famine or prison. Thus, this would negate the main premise.

If you wish to decry BDSM as some sort of barbaric social evil - you are certainly free to do so. I cannot, however, agree.

Your blog is one of the smartest I've read so maybe you can answer my question. I know I want to submit to a man eventually as husband and wife. But all I see on these blogs is oral sex, anal sex and women being beaten and tied up with spit all over their faces. Why don't they show straight up sex in the vagina? I don't want to suck and I am never doing anal. I don't want to be a slapped around or peed on. I just want to be submissive to my husband. Can't I just do that?

———————————~———————————

Thank you for the wonderful compliment and asking me this serious question. I can see you are at the beginning of what I hope will turn into a good journey for you.

First - It seems to me that you are choosing to define your sexual journey by what you are not willing to do, instead of what you are willing to do. That's why all you seem to see is the types of sex depicted you don't want - because you are looking through the eyes of "No." Try looking through the eyes of "Yes" - look for things you do want to do for a man, and you'll see them. There are plenty of pictures of vaginal sex and devotion on this platform.

Second - I think you might be in the right hotel - but wrong hallway. You don't sound very interested in the things that make up the common BDSM experience. You can be a submissive wife without BDSM. My mother and ancestors have done it forever. Perhaps you are seeking what is called a "traditional marriage" or a HOH - "Head of Household Marriage" where the man is in charge and the wife submits but it's just how things are run - not a sexual kink. If you like or desire a little spanking or discipline you might try a Domestic Discipline marriage, or if you are Christian - a CDD (Christian Domestic Discipline) marriage. There are a lot of websites to support both of those ways of living. The sites you mention are for people with more extreme/fetish practices – it's okay if that's not for you. Let it go.

Third - There is a lot of "I will never" in your language. Please remember, the only walls that hold you in are the ones you build yourself. My experience is the less you restrict - even if you end up not doing it - the better. I like a lot of things on my playground. I might not use them all - but I like them to be there just in case.

Fourth - I think you're overwhelmed and possibly out of your league with the sites you've chosen. For one thing —- I'm not sure what sites you look at - but most of the time the stuff on women's faces in these pictures is not spit. :) Dial it back and look at more romantic love or HOH sites.

Does your Master treat you like the fuckmeat cunt you are? I hope he pounds yours holes and spits in your face so you remember you're nothing but a slave and they are only good for fucking.

———————————⁓———————————

Thanks for this brutally descriptive note. I hope writing it gave you much arousal so you could engage in self-pleasure and release your hostility into the tissue closest to your chair.

To answer your question: yes and no. My Master treats me like his property -as I am - but as a valued property - not unlike one would treat a car. He uses me, enjoys me, and doesn't purposely try to wreck me.

He does pound my holes quite roughly for his pleasure. I am grateful, as it is my pleasure also. But he has never spit on me. I don't have any say over that - he just has never chosen to do it. He probably doesn't get aroused by that. He doesn't get off by being disgusting or demeaning.

I am a grateful slave, because while he does spend a considerable amount of time taking pleasure from my body, he has a broader imagination and also engages me on other acts of service that enrich our lives and make us both glad for our relationship.

Women shouldn't be allowed in school. How can you be a slave if you have more education than your Master? You think you're better then you are, smarty-bitch.

———————————————〰———————————————

Thank you for letting me know your opinion. One of the great things about being online is our ability to think differently from one another yet still gather.

I think education is neutral in terms of slavery. Education doesn't make me elevated or free. I am a consensual slave. I have chosen to be lower than all free people and equal to all my sister slaves. Having advanced degrees doesn't change that. What it does do is help me earn more for my family. When I was owned by my husband, the money was his money – I just brought it home and gave him my check on my knees.

Only one of all the Masters who have owned or used me has had the same level of education as I have. Yet, I was underneath them, taking them into my body, crying under their lash and thanking them for using me.

If a slave has an education that does not glorify the slave, but the Master. Only an insecure Master would be afraid to have a well-educated slave.

You said before a session, "When I am very aroused by the prospect of his use I will wear a panty liner at work because I am already wet." Your fear soaking through your clothing? If I was your Master I wouldn't appreciate your shame or hiding the reaction your body has to me. You'd have strict orders to edge in the bathroom and smear your smelly whore juice all over your face and in your hair during work for all future sessions.

———————————~———————————

Dear Anonymous,

You're precious, Sir. What a beautiful fantasy that would be for you in many ways. However, I live in a real world, and in that world -whether or not my Master appreciated me hiding my wetness - my employer would appreciate me being unprofessional at work even less.

I think it is a challenge online for people who live 24/7 on fantasy island where men keep cunts locked in cages and face fuck them at the grocery store - to realize the rest of us - who do this in 3D - in a real way in a real world- have a different way of doing things.

Please enjoy the fantasy from the sidelines. I'll stay on the field where real life happens.

Hey Cunt. I told you to Skype me so I could fuck you and you said no. Slaves don't say no and you ain't no slave. Your a fuckmeat who thinks she's too good for cyber who needs to learn your nothing but a dumb cunt.

Thanks for this note. I would like to take a moment to clarify something and make a helpful suggestion, Sir.

1. I am a consensual slave. I am not YOUR consensual slave.

2. I'm not too good to have cyber-sex with a stranger. I am too honest to have cyber-sex with a stranger.

3. Your = belonging to; You're = you are. Knowing that doesn't keep me from being a dumb cunt. It does keep me from looking like one.

4. I could be wrong, Sir, but I think if you had a different approach to women you do not know than, "Hey Cunt. Skype Me so I can Fuck U in the A$$." You might someday have a sexual experience with an actual person.

I just read your post about your Dom's poker game. It sounds cool but it seems like if they are all your age there would be some flab sticking out or titties hanging low. Some women just shouldn't be naked, you know. Does the quality of the sub factor into who gets an invitation?

———————～———————

Thank you for this somewhat crude and revealing question. I do not know who you are, but your question shows much about your thought process, which is very different from mine, or the Masters who run the game.

Yes, we all are real people in our 40's - not spanking models. There are people (subs and Masters) who are over the recommended weight for their body, and some women with sagging breasts, moles, scars and skin tags. Yet - the nature of fun, service and goodness in the room overrides all of that and no one there notices. The majority feeling in the room is that we would all rather have someone who is real and passionate - no matter what their body type, - than someone who is fake, rude, or judgmental.

It's a group of friends from the kink community here - so the only factor in the invitation is — are you one of the Master's friends who understands the fundamentals of real life submission - including the beauty of every person who bows to serve you?

I'm not thinking you would make the cut.

You said once you don't give road head. But what if your Master commanded you to give him road head. Could you refuse? What would you do? Would you leave him? Because if it means leaving my Daddy over it, I'd probably just do the blowjob and hope for the best.

Nope - I don't give road head (a blowjob to someone while they are driving). I will give one in the car, in a parking lot, at a rest stop - but not while in motion. It's dangerous to myself, my Master and others. It's a limit.

If my Master commanded me to do that, I think I would first look for signs of head trauma - because he wouldn't ask me to do something we both disagree with. But if he seriously wanted me to do that - I would refuse.

I would not leave him over it (although I might ask if we could discuss why he was suddenly violating my limits - since they are pretty broad) - and I would willingly bend over, lay down or take any punishment he wanted to give me for refusing. But I would still refuse.

Certain things (like the pain caused to others through acts of distracted driving) can't be taken back no matter how much you want to. I'd rather take the beating.

If he threatened to release me over it (again, I would look for signs of head trauma) - then it would show he didn't value my service, and it would be time to go.

What about traffic jam head where traffic is really, really slow? Or road handjobs?

Thank you for these clarifying questions.
1. No
2. No
The only thing people need to do when they drive - is drive. Not text, not talk on the phone, and not have sexual stimulation. Just. Drive.

You don't give road head, you don't go ass to mouth, and you don't bareback without a STD test. Maybe you have all these rules because you're just too old for this.

———————⁓———————

Thanks for your somewhat flawed but confident analysis of my situation. I would like to offer you some alternative explanations:

1. I'm in my late 40's…not 400.

2. My nieces also think over 40 is horrifyingly old. They are 12. Similarity?

3. Perhaps these "rules" don't mean I am too old for sexual service. Perhaps they mean I lived to be this old, without disease or injury, because I was smart enough to follow these rules.

You're so practical about everything. Have you ever had a broken heart? What did you do about it?

––––––––––––––––⌇––––––––––––––

Thank you for this question. I'm not sure if you mean the word "practical" as a compliment or not - but I am going to take it as a compliment, because I think to be practical is sometimes a fine thing.

Being a consensual slave - or being in BDSM - doesn't mean we are different from other human beings. It just means we express ourselves and our devotion differently. Of course I've had a broken heart. If you show me someone who has never had a broken heart they have probably never left their house - or they are lying. Heartbreak is part of being real. And part of being me.

Probably the most profound heartbreak was my divorce, and the 2 - 3 years leading up to it. When something that seemed like a perfect fit crumbles in front of you and there is nothing you can do about it - heartbreak is the natural consequence. A profoundly painful event happened to two members of my family whom I love very much, and it created a wound that will never fully heal in them. I ache for them when the memory of it comes back to me. So - yep. Heartbreak.

What did I do? I did what everybody does. I cried. I ate chocolate. I cried some more. I grieved alone and I allowed friends to be present and grieve with me. I picked myself up, and I let others hold my hands. And I did what everyone who has had a broken heart does: I persevered. I learned. I had to learn to move again.

Random Requests

The Slave Speaks

Hopefully by now you know a lot more about me that most people should know about one another, and one of the things I hope you see is my commitment to the BDSM community. When we stop fighting, stop judging and stop needless drama we create a strong place where people can listen, learn, share and grow. In BDSM we live our lives on the edge. We need a safe community to harbor us.

Through this blog I have been able to share my life, my service, my heartbreaks, my joys, my sex habits and my hopes for a better future for us all. I have also been lucky to hear many of your stories, ups, downs, and in-betweens. I have been grateful for every question and conversation I've had online.

To end this book, this section is just a random group of my stories and the stories of others who send me thoughts, questions and situations. I never know what I'm going to see in my inbox on any given day, but there are two things I always know:

1. *I am going to give each "ask" the best answer I can.*
2. *I am thankful someone asked.*

And so to everyone who reads, kneels, commands or follows – I wish you the best of light, life and good service.

Gratitude,

kate

I am 22 and my dream is to find a man who lets me totally serve him by taking care of his house and needs in every way. Men say they want a slave but when I tell them what I want they call me a moocher who just wants to be supported. I know you have your own money but do you think you would be a better slave if you had to depend on your Master and only served him?

———————————∼———————————

Thanks for this question and topic. No, it wouldn't make me a better slave if my Master supported me financially and I had to depend on him. It would make me a captive. This is consensual slavery - it means I am choosing my Master and choosing to stay. If I don't have an education, a job, or a means of supporting myself I am not making a choice - in fact, I have less choices. My Master enjoys me because I choose to serve him based on who he is, not because I need somewhere to sleep and something to eat.

It should be noted that I didn't win the lottery. I worked in high school to get the grades and test scores for a scholarship. I worked in college to keep the scholarship and get a fellowship. I worked at my job to progress to where I am now and I work hard now. All that work is part of what makes me a better slave. I know how to do things I don't want to do because I have to get up in the morning and go to work. I know how to focus on my Master because I had to focus on my homework. I am responsible to my Master because I had to be responsible in life and I can delight my Master because I am educated and well-read.

You may, in time, find a man who desires you to stay at home, keep his house and serve his body — and that would be a wonderful life. Make an investment in your future Master today by getting an education, getting a job, building up savings and learning to stand on your own. Because only when you can stand on your own will a man get the pleasure from being asked to carry you.

I know being judgmental isn't really a good thing. But one thing I've always hated was Masters, etc. who have subs behind their partner's back. It's wrong and hurtful to me. But what are your thoughts about it?

————————————⌒〜⌒⌒⌒⌒/————————————

Thanks so much for sharing your thoughts and asking mine. I love a good discussion. I wish the online format were more inviting of conversation sometimes. It creates community - even when ideas differ.

I think we all see the world through a veil of lace. We have blind spots and we don't see anyone's "whole picture" and so I think it is always better to listen to individuals than judge their acts from afar.

For example - when I was married my husband/Master and I always seemed the "perfect couple" - but we were keeping a secret - that for the last 3 years of our marriage my husband was addicted to prescription drugs and we ended our marriage because after his 3rd failed rehab stay he told me he was choosing the pills over me and I needed to go for both our sakes. I agreed we needed to part. There are many who would say divorce is wrong, or a Master leaving a devoted slave is wrong, but the truth is - divorce was the best thing for both of us. It gave him the chance to hit bottom hard enough to want to change and it freed me from a man who could no longer control himself - let alone Master me. So - every couple has a story you may never know.

Masters who have affairs with subs - it's a hard thing for everyone. Most Masters I know who do it tell me they would rather be a Dom for their wife - but she is vanilla, or isn't sexual at all and won't work out a compromise. So - they feel having a sub on the side keeps them from having to divorce their wife. I know a Master whose wife told him at 38 years old that she didn't ever want to be sexual with him again. He loves her. He loves his kids. He doesn't want to leave. But a lifetime of masturbation isn't good either. In his mindset, the release he finds with his sub allows him to stay married and stay sane. I have a hard time saying he is all wrong. I don't know what it's like to lay by a spouse who won't touch me - but I bet it's horrible.

My Master is married and his wife finds sex painful and avoids it, doesn't care for any form of kink, and doesn't provide oral or hand jobs or much stimulation. Years before he met me - he met a woman online and considered an affair but he decided to tell his wife about it instead and told her if she didn't allow him to dominate someone he was going to have an affair or end up divorcing her. She agreed to let him start by having a spanking only sub - and then it progressed to sex then years later all the way to me and her acceptance of me in her home and in her bed. She told me in the beginning it was such a bitter pill - letting another woman please her husband in a way she couldn't. But now, she feels it a relief. She can enjoy the love they share and not feel the pressure of knowing he was unfulfilled.

But what if she had not agreed? Should he divorce her? What about their love? What about their kids? Should he live a half-life without sex? There are men with wives who have untreated sexual trauma in their past who just sexually shut down. They don't want to leave, and struggle to stay. I don't know the answer for everyone or anyone.

I know it is painful for the partner. And for the sub. And for the Master. I hope Masters who do it try to handle it as wisely and gently as possible. I wish there was a better solution or reality for many couples.

So that's what I think about it. I think it is a three car pile-up waiting to happen, and I hope - always hope -

there's a way to escape the inevitable crash before someone gets irreparably hurt. But it's not my business to tell others where and how to drive.

Those are my thoughts. Thanks again for asking and opening conversations on a serious issue for all of us in this life.

You present such a clear head every time you answer a question on here, and we do get the impression that it must be the same with you in most other situations. This makes me quite jealous of you. But being a random Dom, I can call you slave and you have to call me Sir... This gives me a strange sort of pleasure. In fact, it's even more pleasurable to confide this in you.

—————————————— ～ ——————————————

Thank you, Sir, for your delicious confession. It gives me a tremendous pleasure to walk around each day knowing I am a slave in the presence of free people and treating them as they deserve from one such as myself.

Besides, if you can't enjoy your power, what's the point of having it?

I'm a guy who is submissive to a lesbian who doms guys. I really like worshiping her but now she is trying to get pregnant with me because she and her girlfriend want a kid. She treats me the same but I feel like I'm being used and she doesn't really care about me anymore. I live in a small town and there's not a lot of women who will dom a guy here. What should I do?

————————— ~~~~~ —————————

Thank you so much for writing me and trusting me with your feelings. I am honored you chose to ask for my opinion. First, and always, I want to be clear to respect your Mistress. She is a person in authority over you and I commend her as such.

First things first. I do not know what country you are living in, but you need to check and make sure you understand what the laws are regarding your obligation legally and financially to a child created in this situation. In the United States you can be held legally and financially responsible for this child until he or she is 18. There are forms you can file legally terminating your parental rights and they can sign signifying you have no financial responsibility. Make sure they are signed, and notarized before the child is conceived. Get real forms from a lawyer – not just something they printed up.

Even if someone tells you, "Oh, we won't sue you for child support" – situations change. Ideas change. Legal obligations change. Either be willing to support the child or protect yourself with more than a promise.

After you get all that part done – the feelings. You will find when women are trying to conceive they already have a child in their head – even before he or she is in their body. So you may feel a distancing because your Mistress is more focused on being a mom than a Mistress right now. Or, you may have become overwhelmed with the idea of conceiving a child and your feelings are in a different place right now. You may be resisting the idea, but are in a submissive trance in which you can't really see/say that so your mind is trying to tell you by changing how you feel. The fact you wrote a stranger on the internet and asked for advice means something about this is troubling you.

To me, the best thing to do is ask for permission to speak freely to your Mistress and tell her about your feelings. If she's willing to conceive a child with you, she is hopefully willing to talk to you. Express any concerns, needs, or changing emotions you have about the situation. See what she has to say.

The worst reason to stay with anyone is because you think they "are the only one." – Trust me – there will be another. It may take time to meet her, or you may have to travel. But, don't be involved in something you don't feel right about simply because you think it is the only game in town. The worst decisions we make in life are out of fear.

Trust your instincts, and communicate them as well as you can. Best of luck to you.

I appreciate your personal honesty and the level at which you share, including your age. When I read about the Code d'Odalisque I was struck by how much emphasis is placed on youthful beauty in that form of consensual slavery. Obviously the bloom of youth doesn't last forever but a slave's heart never dies. What are your thoughts about discipline, usage and service as you grow older? How have things changed for you since your twenties?

Thank you so much for your wonderful words and most importantly for this fantastic question. Age is not something we talk about a lot online or in blogs, yet it's something all of us experience.

Personally, I love being in my 40's. I've experienced enough to know what I enjoy and what I don't – and am solid enough in life that I can enjoy my slavery without worrying about the past – or the future. I am free to be me, on my knees. There is a perspective and confidence you get when you grow older and embrace your age and journey – it's very balancing and serene.

As I have grown older, discipline has changed from something I need to something I enjoy. I am a disciplined person – so now it is all about taking the pain/punishment to please the Master and that's much more fun than getting a belting because I got caught speeding. It takes longer to heal, and sometimes longer to stand up after a good hard session – but it's worth it and it feels incredible. We control how "old" our bodies and minds are.

I was a dominated girlfriend in my 20's and that was before there was the internet for popular use – so I felt very isolated and weird (in fact the first time I asked to be spanked my boyfriend called me a "weird girl") and I felt like it was only me who wanted this. I actually went to a therapist about my spanking need because I thought it meant I was immature and "wouldn't grow up and let it go." Now – I am part of a worldwide community of Masters and slaves and it feels good to never be alone.

In my 20's being beautiful was about the cover – not the book. It was a very external – "how you look" kind of thing. Now past 40– beauty is about what is inside – it is about a gentle nature, a giving heart, a sense of humor and the ability to give pleasure.

As women age the biggest issue in slavery is hormones. Some days you are so aroused and needy you beg to be taken roughly and it's all you can think about. Even the stick shift on the car looks good! Then other days – sex is the last thing on your mind and you just want to sit in a hot tub and eat bread, pasta and chocolate all day. The great thing is – both are useful in serving a Master. On those days your hormones are bouncing off the wall – you can offer your Master quite a ride (and encourage him to take several) – on the days you aren't interested – you can focus on obedience, domestic service or get the joy of serving his pleasure just for him. It's a sacrificial act – and that feels amazing to the heart.

I'm a Daddy for an AB/DL. My wife knows, doesn't get it but lets me do it online only. My son married a very religious woman. The other night while at our house my daughter-in-law used my laptop to make a dinner reservation and saw my blog. She got my screen name and later looked at the page. Now she says I can't be around her children because I'm into kids. Do you have any statistics that show Daddies aren't dangerous to real kids. I love my grandkids and can't lose them. My wife is so upset.

Thank you, Sir, for writing and asking my help with statistical evidence. I am a girl who loves numbers and works with them every day. You are correct. There is no statistical evidence or correlation between adults who enjoy adult people in baby role-play and people who fantasize or enact sexuality toward children. Fetish role-play and pedophilia are not connected in any way.

However - stop and think a minute: How are you going to communicate that to your daughter-in-law? You really can't go say, "I talked to a smart woman who said there is no correlation. She's a consensual sex slave I met while reading her porn blog." That won't help.

So here's my thoughts:

First - check yourself. She was gunning for you. She didn't just "happen" upon your Tumblr as she was making a reservation. If I was religious and sat down at my sister's computer to order a pizza, I would Google the place or type in the box. Tumblr just wouldn't appear.

And - if a naughty blog popped up, I would pray, "oh Jesus, please wash out my eyes." Then I would click it off. I wouldn't stare at it or click around it long enough to get your screen name. She was looking for this information. So, you may think you have been "keeping it online" - but it's clear your secret is leaking out.

Second - your wife has every right to be upset. In her mind, it's not bad enough you are doing something she doesn't understand and probably doesn't like - taking time away from her while you do it - but now seeing her grandchildren is in danger. Make communication and reconciliation with her your first priority - Not the grandkids.

Third - the daughter-in-law is never going to hear you. There are no words that are going to make her see that a man having a relationship with a grown woman in a diaper for sexual/personal purposes is okay. So stop trying to win her to your side. Instead - talk to your son and daughter-in-law and say that who you are sexually/personally is really your business and you aren't willing to discuss that part of your life with them. But - you are not dangerous in any way. Offer to see a counselor with them to help them work through the concern fairly so no one has to lose out.

Best of luck and hope to you.

If you spent this afternoon with your Master, how did today's session actually unfold? (Feel free to ignore if this feels intrusive.) You are incredibly generous with your answers--thank you!

———————⟨∿⟩———————

Thank you for your question. I did spend today with my Master and it was challenging and wonderful, then lost as we both fell asleep (I think we've been working too hard).

The challenging part was that after the initial spanking and large plug inserted (along with the penis gag - a favorite) - he tied my legs open and had them turned so the inner thigh was accessible. I was supposed to get 6 cane stripes on each inner thigh - but a few didn't take very well (he wanted 6 clear cut skin welts) so I ended up taking 7 and 10. He took me, while still tied and stinging like crazy - slowly - rubbing his body against the wounds knowing each thrust was burning me but it brought his beautiful cock deep into me - until I was begging behind the gag. I tried lifting my hips - anything to speed up…but he kept going slowly - holding himself against me and eventually toying with my clitoris until I was gasping and rocking beneath him. He withdrew and ejaculated on my caned thighs - sending another wave of stinging pain. His purpose, besides his pleasure, is that for the next few days every time I sweat or move - I'm gonna feel a ghost of that pain. I am so grateful for his delicious and generous nature.

After that, I served him some dessert and coffee, kneeling with my legs open so he could see his good work as he answered some emails. Then he stretched out on the couch and allowed me to hold him in my mouth, sucking and nurturing him. And, he fell asleep. I just continued holding and gently kissing his member and then…I fell

asleep. We woke up an hour later - me first - realizing my
head was still in his lap and my legs were stinging like
mad. (It took me a moment to remember why). I kissed and
nuzzled him until he woke. He put nipple clamps on me
that connect to my collar, and had me dust a curio cabinet
and bookshelf in the room as he continued to watch TV. He
had a second arousal, which he let me drain with my
mouth, fervently bobbing my head back and forth on him.
After thanking him, he told me I could remove the plug and
that I was dismissed. He went back to sleep on the couch (a
second climax knocks him out) and I dressed and came
home for a lovely bath, dinner and night to myself. I feel
my legs every time I move and even now I am sitting very
un-lady like with them wide apart - however tomorrow
when my family is present and I have things to do - I'm
going to have to bring them together, and I will feel it -
deep inside my core.

Would you mind elaborating on what you mean about the poker games and serving at them? How did your Master like you to be in front of groups/friends?

Hi! Thank you for your question and allowing me to be clearer. There is a group of Masters who are friends - largely a social circle - all professional, educated men with slaves, subs or lg's, all of us about the same age - who meet for a poker game.

The game is by invitation only, alternates between houses of Masters who want it there (we do have a few Masters who have wives who do not know about their sub, so the game obviously doesn't go there, and we never hold it in a house where there are children present anywhere on the premises) and each Master brings his servant with him. Some of them have been coming to the game for a long time. My former Master attended regularly and brought me as his servant. My current Master occasionally came to the game – usually with a sub belonging to another Master because he did not have a slave or sub at the time.

Servants (that's easier than typing slaves/subs/lg's) wear a collar, chastity belt, and heels. Sometimes a bustier if her Master prefers. We serve the Masters drinks, bring them snacks, shuffle cards, etc. Other than that –we hang out together in the kitchen and chat with one another, etc. Each Master will take a turn as dealer (just like normal poker). The first time a Master deals he must put the chastity belt key to his servant in the pot as his ante. Whoever wins that pot wins sexual service from that servant at the end of the night. It's not uncommon for a Master to win more than one key – in which case he has more than one woman serve his sexual desires. I always like that because it's fun to serve with my friends. Some Masters won't win any key hands, and they just have to wait for their own slave to be finished with her duty before leaving.

All men wear condoms for all things (including oral) when they are with a slave who is not their own. After the game ends, Masters take the servants whose keys they have won to a bedroom or private corner or designated area (depends on whose house it is), unlock the servant and do with them what they want – and the slave serves their needs. Once they have climaxed, they return the key to the servant and leave (or go wait for their slave to finish up).

My former Master used training to prepare me for sex with men I didn't particularly like or know, and gave me tips on how to serve them and not make it seem like a duty, but a joy. He taught me how to show my devotion to him by serving others well. My current Master won my key several times so I knew I liked and enjoyed him sexually before my former Master told me he was moving and suggested a transfer to my current Master.

My Master does not hold the game at his house because his wife would not enjoy that. It's a shame, because I would love to show off his house and be the "main hostess" for a game – but it's not going to happen. It's just a fun way to get together, share time and enjoy ourselves.

It has been mentioned that you use a chastity belt and that your master holds the key. Which belt do you use, and do you wear it 24/7?

———————～————————

    Thank you so much for this question. Chastity belts are such a great attitude and physical component of slavery. My formal belt (the one I wear under a serving dress when serving in public and at the poker game) is an older Tollyboy FGA/200 that was fitted for me. I also have a more informal adjustable leather chastity belt from Strict Leather which is more comfy.

    I do not wear them anywhere near 24/7 because of family and work concerns. It simply isn't practical. I put one on before going to the Master's for sessions if he asks, or before going to serve him at poker games (always), or whenever he requires.

    Sometimes when I go over to his house to serve him and his wife dinner, or to do some other domestic or personal service, he will ask me to wear it and leave me in it all night or unlock for his use and lock me back (that's the most delicious time -when he uses me, leaves me aroused and needy then locks me back in the belt, knowing there is nothing I can do but suffer). We both have a key to the Tollyboy and there are several keys to the strict leather. Once I get home, I unlock myself and clean and store it. But, I confess, I love being in it and wish I had the kind of privacy/life that allowed me to spend even more time locked. It's the best feeling.

Do you ever socialize with slave friends outside the Dom's poker game--two or three of you having lunch or dinner together, for example? Within your own D/s community how unusual is your arrangement with your Dom and his wife?

~

Thank you for your questions. I love a chance to talk about community.

Yes, I do see slave/sub friends - who are essentially just friends - for lunch or for a drink after work, just like I enjoy time with my vanilla friends. My time is limited these days - but I do try to socialize with friends when possible. Every once in a while we will have a "girl's day out" with a bunch of us who are subs, and get a drink or see a movie. It's fun. Serving a man's needs - particularly if you are hiding your service - can be very lonely. Making friends who "get it" and know what you're going through really helps.

My arrangement - a woman serving a married couple - isn't really unusual at all. I know several slaves who do so and one of my favorite young friends serves a couple. What is a little different is that my Master's wife is not a Domme or Mistress. Many men with vanilla wives either hide their sub (an affair) or keep her away from the vanilla partner. The fact I serve my master and honor his wife as the Lady of the house that owns me is a little different - but it works. That's the baseline question in service decisions –"does it work?"

slave, you wrote it is inappropriate for you to serve with an unspanked behind. Why is that?

───────────────────〜──────────────────

      Thank you, Sir, for asking and allowing me to explain my statement. If we lived in a culture that recognized a slave class, I don't think it would be a big deal. But we don't. We live in a culture largely dominated by equality. So, asserting the difference between a slave woman and a free woman has to be done more intentionally - and visually.

      A slave with a white rear is one who is not serving in her reality. She has the same bottom as a free woman, and may more readily forget she does not have or want the same privileges.

      To be stripped, placed over a lap, bed or couch and spanked until your behind is red reduces the slave - literally taking off the layers of the world. Being reddened - not because you did anything wrong (punishment) or for sex (erotic spanking) but just because you are a slave and that's what happens to slaves, is a powerful re-enforcer to the slave and to the Master about the reality of the service.

      A free woman can wear a collar for fashion, a submissive or little can wear a collar and be spanked (largely punishment or erotic spankings) - however - to be continually red is the hallmark of a slave and much appreciated. Every time the lucky slave sits down on her red behind she gets the pleasure of feeling exactly what she is. What a blessing.

You write how you cannot serve a Master full-time while taking care of your elderly parents. If a Master would find you and help you care for your parents, would you become his slave? Do you worry about being too old to find a Master when your parental care phase is over?

———————————— ⌇ ————————————

  Thanks for your thoughts. Please allow me to answer the last part first so it is clear.

  The Master who only wants a slave who is young is not the Master for me - no matter what age I am. So no, I am not worried about being "too old." I had a slave heart at 20, I will have one at 50 and I'll have one at 80. I'm pretty sure there are Masters who will still be Masters as they age as well.

  In terms of help with my parents - I have been blessed with a fantastic career and have more than enough financially to care for their needs and the rest of mine. I came from a very financially poor family so I'm pretty much the breadwinner for all of us - which is fine.

  The care my parents get from me is living in my guesthouse on my property (although they spend most of their time in my living room), and me making sure they get food and around town and to church and the things they need. When they need intensive medical care- a new solution will present itself. But it's not time for that. My previous Master, (who took a job across the country and moved) understood my time constraints (high-power job, family, etc.) and had me serve him on pre-arranged times/weekends, as it was all the time he had as well. That was a huge bonus. He wasn't sitting around waiting for me to show up and serve — he barely had any time himself so we worked well together. My current Master has much the same ideas.

A Master who would want to help with the physical care of my parents would be a kind and generous Master, and the woman he chose would be a lucky slave. For right now, (which may mean 6 months or 16 years) that slave is not me.

Who in your personal life would be most shocked
if they found out about you being a slave?

────────────────〜────────╱──────────

Thanks for a chance to ponder that. Like most
people with a deeply private side - it's always a curiosity to
wonder what people might say if they found out.

My knee-jerk reaction would be to say "my parents"
- but then as I thought about it - not really. I was brought up
in a home that believed men were the head of the
household, women were born to submit and serve them in
silence and with obedience. So - even though none of their
daughters stayed in the faith - I don't think it would
surprise them to find I was still attracted to that idea. Now,
the sex/spanking part - that would shock them.

My sisters both know about me (one disapproves,
one doesn't care), and I have a lot of Dom/Master or
sub/slave friends so I'm not totally hidden.

I guess the person most shocked would be my
administrative assistant at work. I am very stoic at work. I
don't play, I don't make friends with employees, and I
don't chat. I don't eat in the lunchroom. I'm in charge and
I'm all business all the time. They think I am made of pure
ice. So the idea that I adore nothing less than sexual slavery
or the fact half the time I'm working with fading bruises
and welts under my dress suit - would shock my assistant to
the end of the earth.

Please describe your most humiliating experience
as a consensual slave.

Thank you for this ask. It is actually one of the more
difficult questions for me to answer.   Just like it's almost
impossible to punish a masochist - it is almost impossible
to humiliate a slave. We're slaves! What we are doing isn't
our choice (other than our consensual choice to be a slave)
so it doesn't feel like humiliation - it feels like obeying.

I have had embarrassing things like dropping the
Master's dinner plate in front of guests…but I think you are
probably asking a more sexual question.

The only time I remember feeling like "Wow, this is
humiliating" was one time when we were on vacation out
of town in a hotel. My Master wanted the weekend to be a
sort of "revisit your training" weekend (we did that two or
three times a year - a high protocol/push limits kind of
weekend) - After arriving, my Master gave me a very good
spanking/strapping that left my behind very raw and red,
and inserted a butt plug and large dildo in me and put me
naked in the corner. He ordered room service and then he
ordered me to hold my cheeks open revealing the plug.
When the food came he met the guy at the door and asked
if nudity bothered him. He was a college age man who said
it did not - so he had the guy come into the room and set up
— all the while I was on display. I do remember feeling
very embarrassed that someone vanilla was seeing this. My
Master tipped him and showed him out, then allowed me to
feed him dinner and eat with him.

But - as I said - I did what I was told, so it wasn't
my shame as a slave. If I had said no to the Master - that
would have been shame. I think once you accept yourself -
you don't have that need or arousal in that way. For
example - these women who beg, "Please call me a whore,

tell me what a cunt I am" - on men's blogs. Clearly they get aroused by that humiliation and enjoy it. But it's only humiliating because they think they are better than those words. In their head they are thinking, "I'm a classy woman and he's calling me a whore." When you're a slave and you give up the idea you're better than those words, they don't have the same sexual magic. If a Master says to me, "You're nothing but a fucktoy," my thought is, "Yes."

So - it all depends on perspective.

I like hairy women. Why does everyone on the internet assume slave pussy should be completely shaved? This is wrong. Just wrong.

───────────────⌒───────────────

Thanks for this opinion - it's actually not one I hear often, and it is always lovely to see an opinion asserted so well.

I believe the basic idea is, and it has been a part of my slave practice, that a slave should be shaved at all times to be fully open and visible to her Master. That area is his property and he should be able to see and have access to it at all times. Shaving is also used as a tool to help remind a slave her body is not her own. She can't have hair just because she wants it.

If you are the Master/Mistress, it is fully your right to have a slave with huge tufts of hair. Just command her so. As for the internet - check out older pictures from before the 90's and you'll see more pictures of hairy women, or pictures from Europe where body hair isn't such a big deal.

In all relationships isn't there a natural leader and a natural follower? Why do people find it so weird to define it as Dom and sub?

———————⌒——————

Thank you for your interesting question. Relational dynamics are always fun to think about. Dom/sub implies a lot more than one is leading and one is following. It implies that one has the power and one has given it up. Now, that's not a reason anyone should be offended or freaked out – but human beings often resist what they do not understand.

It is not true that in most relationships there is a natural leader and a natural follower. It happens sometimes (largely relationships structured by religious ideas). Most vanilla relationships practice an equality of opportunity and experience. For example, in a married couple – the wife may be a better money manager than the husband, so she pays the bills. She's not the leader of the whole marriage, but she is the leader of monetary decisions. A husband may be a better cook or interested in cooking – so he does the dinner. It's not about one being in charge of the other – but who does what best.

In Dom/sub there is an intentional power exchange, where one person gives up the rights to be empowered to the other person no matter what skill set or circumstance. That is very different. There is also a sexualized component and a discipline component in D/s most relationships in the vanilla world don't sustain. So – for people on the outside of this life – Dom/sub seems odd, scary, or wrong – because they don't get it. That doesn't make it wrong and it doesn't make them bad people. It just means there is a gap of experience there – and it is hard to overcome.

I saw you said you were having a subs night out today. That sounds so hot. Do you all wear collars or bracelets or something to show you're subs. Maybe go without underwear or in stockings? Do you talk about what you do with your Masters? Maybe after a few drinks you go to a subs house and make out a bit. What if you didn't have permission to play with the others? Would you text your Master to ask if you could? Just this once?

Wow… thanks so much for your questions and sharing your sexual fantasy with me. It seems you know how women in porn movies act, but not how real life subs behave.

A group of us are taking a sub friend whose husband is very ill out for a "night out dinner." We are wearing casual clothes (I'm wearing jeans and a sweater), and relaxing. We are going to a steakhouse, where we will spend time catching our friend up on work stories, movies, funny stories (probably a little Master talk there), and garden plans. We will hug each other, leave a nice tip for the servers, get in our cars and go home by 9.

Thinking about kinky fun is great. But in the real world - sometimes dinner is just dinner.

It seems like you are a part of a great community of like-minded individuals who love their lifestyle. I'm curious though, in all the years you've been in and around the BDSM life, have you seen women you suspected were non-consensual slaves or subs? Or, Doms who were excessive for your taste??

―――――――――――~――――――――――

     Thank you for this question. It is a sad and yet clear reality of any community - the church community, the arts community and the BDSM community that abuse happens. I have certainly seen bad things occur.

     In one instance when I was still married, a woman who was a sub of a friend of my husband's came to us and said she was being battered and was afraid to leave. She had called the police when he was beating her but he told the police they were a kink couple (and they certainly had a houseful of stuff to prove it) so the cops told him that if she called them again they would have to intervene and they left. We did what anyone would do. We let her hide in our vacation cabin for a few days and arranged to pick up her stuff. Since my husband was involved her Master didn't fight us. We took enough pictures and evidence for her to get a warrant of protection and she ended up moving in with her family in another state.

     In the excessive Dom category - almost 3 years ago when I was still pretty newly owned by my current Master, another Master started bringing a sub to the games who was young and new to the life. She never complained. But, another slave's Master won her one night, and he told his slave that when he had sex with her - he went very gently and she clung to him and cried like she was desperate for love and kindness. Over a few months we watched her esteem crumble, noticed wounds that had no aftercare, and heard needless cruelty come out of her Master's mouth. It clearly wasn't part of any agreement.

The slave whose Master asked us to check it out, my friend and myself went to our Masters and asked them to be a voice for her. They ended up asking the abusive Master to come to Janice's house. We three knelt beside each of our Masters as silent witnesses and the Masters told him they felt he was being abusive and unacceptable. The Master admitted that he didn't like the girl anymore, was bored with her, and didn't know how to get rid of her. So they gave him ideas about how to humanely release her.

Abuse is not the norm in BDSM. Safe, sane and consensual is the norm. But - it does occur sometimes. When consensual slaves see abuse - it is best to share it with their Masters - as they have a better chance of intervention — but it is important to never turn a blind eye when any being - animal, or human, is being harmed.

Have you ever met a male slave? Is that weird for you? How do you feel about BDSM forums?

———————〜———————

　　Thanks for your questions. I have some male friends who are slaves and a friend I met online who is a male slave to his wife (I call him my brother-slave). I have never served beside a male slave, but I think it is something I might like to try someday if someone in my group of friends ends up with a male slave. I think it would add a very interesting dynamic to our group of sister slaves.

　　No, it is not weird for me. Everyone has their own thing - and I don't judge or ridicule that — just because it is not a part of my world, doesn't mean it is not a part of the world. I would never care for a male subservient to me personally (as a slave there is nothing more awkward than someone wanting me to lead or be over that person) - but serving is serving and we could probably find a lot of common experiences.

　　I think BDSM forums are a fine way for people - particularly people who can't be socially open about their kinks - to meet others and create community. I find it a better experience if people just share experiences, encouragements and fun - and skip the drama, name calling and BS.

I love your blog - thank you for sharing it with all of us. I am male and very interested in kink lifestyle (I am perhaps a switch who definitely leans more Dom) but I also have a decent professional standing in a conservative field in a large city that seems rather small at times. How does one go about meeting like-minded people without running the risk of inadvertently outing one's self in a non-tolerant professional community? Do you have any experience with navigating this terrain?

———————————————

Thank you so much for asking. I have a lifetime worth of experience in navigating a professional environment that is highly scrutinized while maintaining kink life. Everyone has their own ways of protecting their identity and not everyone will like or agree with all of mine - however, I am responsible for my safety and my choices answer only to that and my Master who uses the same choices.

1. If possible, play out of town or start community with folks out of town. You may find other people you know in the kink scene there - but if they are playing in another place - they are just as concerned as you are.

2. Use online environments for getting to know people and spend time checking them out. Don't take anything they say at face value. Ask questions, verify their answers and spend time (don't meet someone after the second email and NEVER give them personal identifiers until you are sure about them (wait weeks).

3. Develop a persona that is you, but not identifiable as you. DO NOT lie about who you are. Do not make up a

person and catfish others. But, do give yourself a different name.

      4. Do not post pictures of yourself or anything that would identify you. I get requests to post dresses I wear, my shoes, my body with the face blurred out - but anyone who works with me or sees me socially is going to know that's my dress, or birthmarks or shoes. So - as much as I would like to - and as much as I admire those who can — no pictorial evidence. It's fine if someone at work or a social board "thinks" I'm kinky. It's not okay if they can prove it.

      5. Don't use your personal cell phone (and for god's sake don't take penis pics with it) for your activities. Throw-away phones are around 20 bucks, and have all kinds of options and services, from pre-paid to subscription. Get a throw-away for play, pics, and other stuff. Don't connect that phone to facebook, etc. That keeps an untrustworthy person from using/publishing your number or tracking you - -and makes sure your lovely cock or a picture of you beating a nipple clamped woman with a flogger doesn't end up on facebook when someone steals your phone.

      6. Play big but stay small and exclusive (this is where I get the hate mail from) - Develop a network of kink friends you trust and stick with that group. Keep your personal kink community small, and only allow people you trust who have as much understanding of your professional needs as you do. Our group of friends has known each other for years. We all have the same level of education, employment, social commitment, and responsibility. So - we all understand discretion. It doesn't make me a snob that I only serve and play with people like me whom I trust. It makes me protected and smart.

      The world is full of people who say "This is my kink and I'm not ashamed and I don't care who knows it." That's good for them. I have a job that is supporting my

family. I don't have that privilege. I do care who knows.
Make the best decisions for you and don't be teased,
tempted or bullied out of them.

I need your grace to remind me to find my own.

What a beautiful note. Thank you so much.

Truth is - we all need each other to encourage the better angels of our nature.

About the Author

When she's not reviewing research statistics, sitting in a community board meeting or helping her elderly parents carry their groceries, Kate Ashland can usually be found kneeling before her Master wearing nothing but a collar and a smile. Kate is a highly educated executive, department chair, community volunteer, dutiful daughter, loving aunt, compassionate friend, and a BDSM consensual slave. With twenty years of practice as a spanked girlfriend, a submissive partner, an odalisque and a consensual slave, Kate has more than opinions and answers – she has experience. Kate's blog, *Serving as Nature Intended,* is a collection of her ideas, philosophies, experiences and advice for others who want to "find their freedom through consenting submission and service."

Ask Kate

Sometimes Kate's work brings up more questions than she answers. If you have a question/comment for Kate please feel free to email her at: KAshland@heronswing.com

If you would like to ask her anonymously, you can use the button on her blog, *Serving as Nature Intended,* (18 Years or Older, NSFW) or use the form on the author's page at the Heron's Wing Website:

Please be aware: all notes go directly to Kate and will be anonymous. Because it is Anon, she cannot answer you directly. She will answer your question on her blog and it may appear in her next book. Any question or comment that breaks US Law regarding free speech or is a threat she will turn over to the proper authorities.